CITIZENS' BR

A Radical Agenda for

By Paddy Ashdown MP

To Jennifer   Best wishes.

Paddy Ashdown

London · Fourth Estate

First published in Great Britain in 1989 by
Fourth Estate Limited
Classic House
113 Westbourne Grove
London W2 4UP

British Library Cataloguing in Publication Data
Ashdown, Paddy *1941-*
    Citizens' Britain: a radical agenda for the 1990s.
    1. Great Britain. Social conditions
    I. Title
    941.085'8

ISBN 1-872180-45-0

Typeset by York House Typographic, London W7
Printed & bound by Richard Clay Ltd, Bungay, Suffolk

Contents

Acknowledgements

It has taken me a long time to assemble this very personal agenda for change. Its framework and the ideas in it have changed a great deal as I have groped towards a shape and content with which I could be satisfied. In this process I have been greatly assisted by a number of close friends and colleagues.

Among these have been Alan Leaman, with whom I have worked, to my exclusive advantage, for nearly a decade; Richard Holme, whose ideas and insights have always provided me with a different, sharper, view; Bill Jordan, who, because I wrote congratulating him on a book of his, came to help me with mine; Charles Handy whose fresh thinking has always proved such an inspiration to me (and it shows!); David Marquand, whose own book, *The Unprincipled Society* did so much to crystallise my own thoughts and fill in the gaps I could not fill; Peter McGregor, whose thinking on industrial matters has helped me so much; Keith Bradley, who has given me his advice over a number of years; Gillian Gunner and Linda Siegle, who have never given up on educating me on the woman's perspective of our society, even though I have given them good cause; Tony and Theo Beamish, who first introduced me to the *Taylor Nelson Monitor* and who, with Tom Burke, have provided the constant stimulation of new ideas from the environmental agenda; Mark Payne for his views; Olly Grender for her suggestions on quotations; Caroline Barber for her constantly cheerful help; my wife Jane, for her forbearance and advice; my fellow Social and Liberal Democrat MPs for their helpful comments (especially Alex Carlile for his help on law reform); and last, but perhaps most important of all, my wonderful secretary, Alison Nortcliffe, whose tireless and uncomplaining retyping of my numerous redrafts was accomplished with such skill and speed.

None of these bears an atom of adverse responsibility for what is written here — that is solely mine. But all, in their own way, have made the enterprise possible and ensured that the finished product is at least better than it would otherwise have been.

Foreword

LORD GRIMOND

Congratulations to Mr Ashdown on this book. The public need to know where he stands and in it he tells them. It is not an encyclopaedia of party policy. That is right. He points to the direction in which he would like the party to go.

Mr Ashdown remarks on the 'Citadel' aspect of today's Britain – the barriers which divide us – and contrasts it with the 'Citizens'' Britain which he wants us to create. He wants the barriers broken down so that information, participation and wealth are spread. The contrast between Citadel and Citizen is well taken. He is primarily interested in the activities which make up the day-to-day lives of citizens – work, housing, social services and those policies about such matters as the law and the environment which immediately impinge on every day life. There is little about fiscal and financial policy.

It is essential that Social and Liberal Democrats should not only state their ideals and take up a firm political stance but should be clear about the situation in which we are. They can then be clear about the questions that they must answer and the mischief they have to meet. Mrs Thatcher's Cabinet does not believe in small government, less regulation, lower taxation, the spread of wealth and power and competition. On the contrary, under her, corporatism (a polite word for fascism) has spread wide and deep. Statutes and regulations pour out in ever greater quantity. Taxation and the percentage of the national wealth taken by the public authorities are higher than ever. Wealth and power are concentrated. Monopoly capitalism and inflation flourish. With this has come the erosion of free standing institutions such as universities, the degradation of our services and the steady advance of bureaucratic blight.

By removing some unpopular features of their programme the Labour Party does not provide an alternative to either Thatcherism or their own state socialism. It is for the new party to offer a third way.

With this book in hand, the Social and Liberal Democrat leadership should apply itself to deciding upon the main evils and issues it wants to tackle. Having established its stance and where it will make its main thrust it should set about tapping the reservoir of new thought – not forgetting the most important American contributors such as Professor James Buchanan and Martin Weitzman. As Mr Ashdown has shown we cannot live by committees and research assistants alone.

Time is short and the difficulties are great. The press are not as a rule interested in new political ideas, least of all from small parties, but we must remember that the General Election campaign will begin about eighteen months from now. Every effort must be concentrated on essentials and getting them over to the public.

Mr Paddy Ashdown's book is the starting point for this process.

Preface

Most of the New Liberals like Hobson, Haldane, Hobhouse, Samuel and Churchill did not criticise the old Liberalism to destroy it, but rather to interpret it. They admired the heritage of Liberalism, but felt that it ought to be brought into line with the needs of the time. This led to a series of qualifications and readjustments of certain basic concepts, such as responsibility, liberty and citizenship.

Raymond Plant and Andrew Vincent writing on the New Liberals of
the 1890s in *Philosophy, Politics and Citizenship*

I started the thinking which has led to this book on the night of the 1987 general election. I had won my seat, with an increased majority, but across Britain some of my colleagues and many of those I admired had lost. The dream we shared about bringing a new kind of politics to Britain was smashed. I knew that it would not be good enough now simply to re-furbish our old ideas. Like my Liberal forebears of the 1880s and 1890s, we were going to have to do some radical re-thinking; to re-apply the old, timeless liberal principles to the new age and, in so doing, to find the policies which face up to Britain's needs as we approach the turn of the century.

The proposals contained here are not intended as definitive policies, still less a manifesto. They are intended, rather, as a sketch of that new approach – a starting point for discussion, both inside my party and also, I hope, outside its ranks.

In writing this I have been much influenced by *Our Different Vision: Themes and Values for Social and Liberal Democrats*, published in February 1989. The first paragraph stated:

> The challenges which lie ahead reflect form interlocking sets of changes – changes in the pattern of production, both in our society and in the world as a whole; changes in the world economy and in the system of international relations; social and demographic changes, which are in turn changing the structure of our population, and creating new divisions in our society; and changes in attitudes and assumptions, reflected in new ways of thinking, new aspirations and new demands.

It is to those new ways of thinking that this book is dedicated.

Paddy Ashdown was born in India in 1941, brought up in Northern Ireland and educated at Bedford school. Between 1959 and 1972 he served as a Royal Marines Officer. A gifted linguist, Paddy Ashdown went to Hong Kong in 1967 to study Mandarin Chinese. Returning to England in 1970 he was given command of a Commando Company in Belfast. He was, at that time, the youngest Royal marines officer to receive such an appointment since the war.

After 1972 Paddy Ashdown joined the Foreign Office. He was posted to the British Mission to the United Nations in Geneva, where he was responsible for Britain's relations with a number of United Nations organisations and was involved in asepcts of the European Security Conference (the Helsinki Conference).

Leaving the Foreign Office in 1976 he went on to work in local industry in the Yeovil area. He worked first for Westland and then with the Morlands subsidiary, Tescan, which closed down in 1981. After a period of four months unemployment he got a job with Dorset County Council Youth Service, where he was responsible for initiatives to help the young unemployed.

In the same year he left the Foreign Office and joined local industry he stood as Liberal candidate for Yeovil. In the 1979 election he raised the Liberal vote to the highest ever level and won the seat in the 1983 election. In 1987 he further increased his majority. Shortly after entering parliament he was appointed Liberal Spokesman on Trade and Industry affairs. He became Education spokesman in January 1987 and leader of the Social and Liberal Democrats in July 1988. He is currently the Party's spokesman in Northern Ireland and was appointed Privy Councillor on 1 January 1989.

He and his wife, Jane, have been married since 1962. They have two children, Kate aged 24 and Simon aged 21.

Part One
The Choices

There is nothing more difficult to take in hand, more perilous to conduct, or more uncertain of success than to take a lead in the introduction of a new order of things, . . . because the innovation has for enemies all those who have done well under the old conditions, and but lukewarm defenders in those who may do well under the new.

Machiavelli, *The Prince*

1

Introduction

May you be condemmed to live in interesting times

Chinese Saying

We are living through a period of profound and accelerating change in our society. Yet the political debate at Westminster and in the old political parties is not primarily about the sort of future that we want for our country. Both the Conservative and Labour parties are talking about how best to cope with the damage of the past. Neither is talking about the new sort of future that Britain needs.

In this book I have tried to look at the challenges which face Britain and the world in the next decade. I identify some of the options before us and propose a framework for the new shape of progressive politics in the post Thatcher era.

The tenth anniversary of Mrs Thatcher's entry to Downing Street provoked an enormous outpouring of analysis and argument. One message seemed clear, whether from those favourable to the Government or not. After ten years in power, the main framework of Thatcherite thinking is in place. But it is now a spent force. Although the Government is pushing ahead with further ideological reforms to the NHS and with the privatisation of key utilities such as water and electricity, there is an unmistakable air of a revolution which is running out of steam. The debate will soon be no longer about the ingredients of Thatcherism, but will become a debate about Thatcherism's limitations and its contradictions. The test for opposition parties will be to convince the electorate that they know not just where the Thatcherites went wrong but how they can build a better Britain in the years to come.

Some opposition politicians, chiefly in the Labour Party, will be tempted to return us to the collectivist, corporatist thinking of the past. Some will want to reinvent a mythical consensus which, they will say, governed Britain successfully before the Thatcherite aberration. They will try to ignore the need for radical reforms in the way that Britain is governed and in the role that government adopts. In short, they will want to defend the pre-Thatcher past, rather than address themselves to the post-Thatcher future.

I do not believe that the public will respond to such a muted and uncertain call. Britain will not return to the collectivist, corporatist structures of the past. But, as most now realise, neither can a decent future for our country lie in a society built on materialism, selfishness and greed.

The task I have set myself in this book is to suggest an approach to solving an enduring conundrum: how to build a society and a system of government that can provide both individual freedom and social justice.

2

The Future

Yesterday is not our's to recover, but tomorrow is our's to win or lose

Lyndon B Johnson

The future is influenced by new technology, new economic structures and new social problems. But it is not determined by them. These new factors may shape the options but we make the choices.

Britain is facing some complex and major questions which demand clear answers, but which are not getting them.

Are we prepared to commit ourselves wholeheartedly to a European future? Do we have a clear idea about the role of government in the late twentieth century? What is happening to the Welfare State? How can individual liberty be protected in a technological and complex world? What can governments do to improve economic performance? What are the constraints that must be put on freedom in order to meet the ecological threats which now place in jeopardy the very planet on which we live? Is our democracy strong enough to meet the demands that are being placed on it? The greatest danger is that we drift into the 1990s with no clear idea of where we want to go. Our political history is over full of progressive parties who knew what to do to get into office, but had no idea what to do once they were there.

Below I draw two pictures of how Britain could develop, each dependent on the decisions we take. They are not intended as an exercise in futurology; their purpose is to highlight some of the major policy dilemmas we will face in the remaining years of this century.

3

1999 In Citadel Britain

The danger of the past is that men became slaves. The danger of the future is that men may become robots.

Erich Fromm

The Citadel

The classical facades and glittering glass skyscrapers of our capital, and our major cities, provide the offices of our financial empires – banks, insurance companies, pension funds, the headquarters of international enterprises. They also house our government departments, which guard the state. These form the tightly linked power centre of society, monopolising communications, information and control, giving high priority to security, both internal and external. The highest levels of finance, government and the security apparatus have used their access to advanced technology as the means of increasing their power at the expense of wider society, fusing their systems in recognition of their common concerns. This citadel of power is characterised by suspicion and secrecy, thinly veiled in public relations disinformation and evasive ministerial statements. Ministers and decision makers themselves are cut off from the grubby public. Official cars and a *cordon sanitaire* of functionaries stand between them and the slashed seats on the underground, the graffiti and faeces in the underpass and the pavement strewn with hamburger boxes. For them, through the tinted (and discreetly reinforced glass) of the 1999 equivalent of the Daimler Sovereign, the world looks different. Nationalistic in its stance towards the world, Citadel Britain nevertheless adopts opportunistic policies within the global economy, seeking only the highest short term gains from international investment and trade.

Screwdriver Industry

Although the economy still produces rich profits for some, Britain's industrial base has continued to shrink. Those industries which thrive on high technology, creative innovation and adaptive skill have declined. Because education and training have been neglected, Britain has not been able to keep pace with competition from America, Western Europe, Japan or the newly industrialised countries (NIC). More and more products with high capital input, high skills and high added value are being imported. British industry is characterised by assembly plants, where workers with few skills and little training do a screwdriver job for overseas companies or local firms. In our low productivity economy, workers' standards of living and skills lag behind those of other countries, as does the quality of their products. Britain competes for investment with the newly industrialising countries of the Third World. It tries to attract new plants from overseas companies looking for weak planning controls, weak trade unions and workers willing to undertake long hours for low pay. British industry is distinguishable from the rest of Europe by poor training, low skills, low investment, poor working conditions, continuing high overtime and an archaic management style.

Rent a Mop Services

As the gap between rich and poor has widened, the rich can afford to pay for more personal services. Overall unemployment has fallen, but there are pockets where labour shortages persist. Low pay is very common, especially in the service industries. More households have nannies,nurses, maids, cooks, cleaners and gardeners. The leisure industries, in particular, employ casual labour on a large scale. Few of the people in these categories get paid enough to meet their basic needs, but they are able to claim means-tested benefits to bring them above the poverty line.

Just as public services have been privatised, so the largest sector of employment has become private services. The scope for productivity increases in this sector is so low that firms can compete and be profitable only by employing short term part time casual labour. Most of those in this casual sector do not have pension rights, sick pay, holiday pay or redundancy protection. Typically, these workers are married women or young people living with their parents, since wages are insufficient and too unreliable for the 'main earner' in a household.

Private Life

Citadel Britain boasts of family life as its centrepiece, and claims as its foundation the self-reliant, self-responsible household each in its own 'castle'. But behind the security-locked front doors all is not so rosy. Ordinary families experience a good deal of stress during their working lives and increasing anxiety and fear as old age advances. Unable to afford insurance against the hazards of disability, and lacking the support of public services, the growing elderly population increasingly depends on the next generation for help and support. The burden falls unfairly on women expected to give unpaid assistance, or take their parents in, while still trying to sustain the part-time earnings on which household income depends.

The strain on mental and physical health is considerable, and the social costs are high. Women feel themselves increasingly subordinate, excluded and exploited; their paid and unpaid labour is required, yet they are not getting their share of power or income in Citadel Britain.

Meanwhile, whilst the majority of opera, concerts, art galleries and theatre can only survive with the patronage of business for the benefit of the few, the vast majority in Citadel Britain are wholly in the grip of the 'Jumbo culture'. There is little reading and almost no access to conventional culture for the ordinary person. All of these are replaced by the surrogate of soap operas, in which there is an almost ritualised national preoccupation.

Public Perils

Every city has its deprived areas, where the poor and dispossessed live. Despite the apparent general prosperity, a significant minority have been left out. Black people in particular (survey after survey shows that they have lower paid jobs and poorer housing) are disproportionately numerous among the poor who depend on state benefits and state services for their living. Although there are skill shortages in many areas, unemployment in these districts remains high because whole households are unable to afford to work.

High travelling and child care costs combine with low pay and means tested benefit withdrawal, to make it impossible for such people to improve their situation. Many of them feel that their only alternative is fiddling, hustling and crime.

As a result state officials maintain a brooding and coercive presence in these areas. Employment officials try to enforce low paid work under threat of benefit withdrawal; taskmasters supervise 'workfare' schemes for cleaning streets and public buildings; offenders are engaged in 'punishment in the community', doing similar tasks, monitored through electronic tags. All residents carry identity cards; relations with officials are tense and volatile; community relations are hostile; curfews for the young are in force; while the police are seen as protecting some, they are regarded as persecuting others. Coercion and control are part of the experience of daily life.

All over the country, the public environment has become shabby, down at heel and dangerous. Public transport is so unreliable, comfortless and risky that it is used only by the poor, while roads are congested and private motorists live with endless delay and frustration. The vulnerable avoid using all public amenities and increasingly stay behind locked doors at night. Some of the young and robust find expression for their frustration and surplus energy in loutish, drunken and violent outbursts. The environment is polluted, crime rates are high; the quality of public resources, public health and public behaviour continue to sink.

Politics

The government of Citadel Britain is built on its outdated political system. The concentration of power in Whitehall is very convenient and whichever political party is in power uses it to maintain its grip on authority. For many years Parliament has been used to acting as a servant of the executive, ensuring that the government of the day gets its way. The power of the state to control the release of information

and to crack down on dissent is greatly aided by the absence of a
Statute of Rights and an enfeebled official opposition which, willing
to wait its turn for power, always plays its politics by the conventional
rule book. Meanwhile, more and more citizens are disillusioned with
the political choices available to them and turn out has fallen consistently at elections to the point where Parliament has decided to make
voting compulsory. Nevertheless, the standing of Parliament continues to fall in the public esteem.

Regionally, too, Britain has become a nation of citadels. Many
within the citadel walls, especially in the south and east, enjoy
security and prosperity. Many more are outside, banging at the gates
to get in.

4

1999 In Citzens' Britain

Some people see things that are and ask themselves 'Why?'. I dream things that never have been and ask myself 'Why not?'

Aeschylus

Democratic Society

In Citizens' Britain, it is the people's homes in all their rich if untidy diversity, which have become the real centres of power. Information technology has not been used to concentrate power but to disperse it. Government has taken active steps to give all citizens access to new communications systems, giving people more control over their own lives and over the organisations which influence them. Decision makers, both in government and out of it have recognised that the best structure for managing and governing is one which does not concentrate power but disperses it, and enables a teamwork rather than 'top-down' approach. Workers have more knowledge and power in their workplace. Many own their own jobs and are self employed. Every person owns an economic stake in the nation's economy, through a universal share ownership programme, the Citizens' Trust. Similarly, all citizens have a share in the ownership of the privatised utility industries which serve their needs. Citizens participate more fully in government. Emphasis is on openness and rights of access, on sharing information, not guarding it; on discussion not secrecy. A reformed legal system gives each citizen on equal access to justice, with a Statute of Rights to protect freedoms. Internationally, Britain, an active participant in an increasingly integrated Europe, is seen as a promoter of constructive co-operation. We enjoy good relations with Eastern Europe, many of whose nations have taken affiliated status with the EEC. We are also leaders in international moves to solve global problems such as environmental destruction, disease and famine.

Adaptive Industry

British industry is adapting to new conditions through the benefits of political commitment to education and training. Taking its lead from Europe, Britain has invested in a crash programme to improve standards, especially in higher and adult education. Many people retrain or 'up-skill' twice or more in their working lives. Education has moved away from early specialisation to establishing a broad base on which specialist skills can be built. Distance learning, especially through the use of information technology, has become far more widespread, particularly in adult education. There is a thriving high technology sector of industry. A skilled workforce earns high wages through producing good quality products.

The labour process is much more varied and flexible in Citizens' Britain. In many enterprises, a relatively small core of permanent headquarters staff manage the work of employees who are dispersed, some working on a self-employed basis from their own homes and some in small decentralised units. This is not simply to save costs; it also gives workers greater autonomy and a better quality of life. Men and women are more able to share unpaid household work and child care, and both work part-time when there are major caring duties to share. People place a higher premium on adequate pay with adequate leisure than on high pay for long hours. Quality of life has become just as important as large wage packets. Indeed emphasis has shifted from overall levels of pay to a greater concern with net levels of disposable income. With more frequent retraining, the idea of sabbatical periods away from full time employment has become more accepted.

Income Security and Employment

As part time work increases, and a variety of employment contracts develops, the rights and protection of those workers becomes a matter of concern. Employers and trade unions value these 'irregular' as well as regular workers, and seek to advance their interests. The government adopts an income maintenance system which encourages part time work and flexibility – a Basic Income, which gives security to each individual. Although this seems controversial at first, (because it guarantees a tax-free income to each citizen irrespective of work or marital status) it is soon recognised as encouraging enterprise, self-employment and a rational use of technology and human energies. It also provides an income for periods of training and advanced education. The Basic Income gives unskilled workers far better opportunities and incentives in the labour market than a means-tested benefits system. Every citizen also receives an annual, if at first limited, dividend from the shares held in a Citizens' Unit Trust and in the privatised utility industries. They understand that clean water and unpolluted air are essential to their own health and that of their children. Meanwhile, conditions of work, security of employment and pay bargaining are increasingly seen to be protected better through employee rights and profit sharing than through trades union rights and government legislation. Most workers in Britain have a share in the ownership of the firms in which they work.

A Healthy and Caring Society

In Citizens' Britain people are concerned about quality of life, and not just about quantity of material possessions. They want to live a healthy and fulfilled life, to take an interest in what they consume and in self care. They use information technology to monitor their own health, and expect professionals and experts to act as advisors and consultants, rather than taking all decisions for them.

As people live longer, the proportion of elderly and disabled citizens rises. Neither the traditional 'solution' of institutional care nor the alternative of unpaid family care is acceptable. People with disabilities (of whatever age) are not willing to be 'put away' in hospitals, nor to be cut off from contact with their community. And married women, whose skills are in demand for paid employment, want choices which extend beyond low-paid menial work in institutions or accepting the assumption that they will be full time unpaid carers in the family home. So new approaches to care, which respect the autonomy and aspirations of people with disabilities, which support the carers, and which allow women the same opportunities for participation in society as men, are encouraged by state policy.

Community and Citizenship

In Citizens' Britain, people increasingly recognise the importance of an active life as members of a community, and the value of shared resources. They prize their association with others in voluntary organisations, clubs and groups, and their membership of cultural and religious communities. They value good relations between races and faiths. Central and local government promote co-operation between citizens, providing communal facilities for a good quality of life. Environmental protection is a high priority, locally, nationally and in the international community.

Citizens have learnt to place a greater value on shared public amenities, allowing a better balance between private and public, owned and shared, quantity and quality. Public transport and public services are properly resourced, being recognised as a part of the common wealth and essential elements in a good society. It is recognised that the question 'Who owns?', which dominated the debate about public services and utility industries in the 1980s, is less relevant than the question 'How is the citizen served?'. A single powerful watchdog body acts as guardian of the consumer interest where monopolies (state or private) or near monopolies operate in the public sector. Elsewhere consumer power, buttressed by rights to information, guarantees of quality and access to redress, dominates in the market place.

The need to protect and improve the environment is recognised as being central to all the decisions taken in Britain and millions of people spend part of their spare time helping to preserve our natural and cultural heritage.

5

The Choice

Some people may prefer Citadel Britain. After all, the idea of a citadel has associations of achievement, personal security, power and wealth. There are attractions in the distant vista of a shining city on a hill – just so long as we can ignore the swamps around it and the fortifications which protect against those outside its gates. For some, the danger and conflict in that scenario give it more spice and savour. They feel the sense of their own worth most keenly when they can compare their success with others' failure, their possessions with others' poverty, and their status with others' stigma. For these people, and there are more of them than there used to be in Britain, there is little point in reading further. They are unlikely to find anything attractive in this book.

For myself, I prefer Citizens' Britain. For it is the way to deliver the two qualities to which I am dedicated so passionately in politics – individual liberty and social justice.

My task in this book is to show that this is a realistic scenario for the future, and that we can make it happen. It is also to show why I think we should choose to take this direction. I shall argue that Citizens' Britain is not only desirable but possible. I hope to demonstrate that it can be a stimulating, forward looking, realistic society, not just a worthy aspiration.

6

Constructing Citizens' Britain

Mankind has become so much one family that we cannot ensure our prosperity except by ensuring that of everyone else. If you wish to be happy yourself, you must resign yourself to seeing others also happy.

Bertrand Russell

The essence of modern citizenship is its acceptance of interdependence, and interdependence forms one theme of this book. This is not intended as a series of bright ideas thrown together in a kaleidoscopic fashion, but as a closely woven, coherent set of concepts designed to form the network for a sustainable and caring society for the new age.

The book is, itself, constructed like a network. It works like this:

Linking Principles

A network needs something – bonds, links, ties – to hold the elements together.

In this book, the bonds are linking principles which bind together all the citizens in society. In Part Two I outline these principles, and say how they could provide a new kind of political community in which everyone has a stake in Britain and in the better quality of life it could sustain.

Policy Threads

A network must also be joined through some medium.

In Part Three I outline the policy threads which hold the network together. Each policy section is divided in two. In the first part, I define the problem and in the second I make some specific policy proposals.

Recurring Themes

Lastly, a network needs reinforcement. The links must be multifaceted; the threads must criss-cross and interweave. The messages must be consistent and mutually reinforcing.

Throughout the book certain themes appear and reappear in every policy area. These themes connect the principles (or foundation ideas) with the policies. They are intended to give the whole a coherence and sense of direction by echoing and reinforcing each other in different spheres. Here are some of the themes, and examples of their relevance.

Protect the Environment Citizens' Britain recognises that the urgent need to protect and enhance our fragile living space is now one of the most important constraints both on public policy and on individual liberty. There are only two short sections in this book specifically on the environment. This is as it should be. For a true acceptance of the environmental imperative is not expressed merely through 'bolt on' policies for more waste bins and recycling plants – it has, as in this book, to inform and influence all policy areas. One point needs to be made here, however. Many in the modern Green movement see environmentalism as a return to a largely mythical pre-industrial past. I see it as the prerequisite for a successful 'third wave' industrial future.

Indeed, I am constantly struck by the correlation between those actions which we would like to take in order to respond to the environmental challenge and those actions we must take in order to achieve success and prosperity in the new industrial age: both require a move from a high resource use/low value added industrial base to a low resource use/high value added one; both require devolved structures of government and management; both require the highest levels of energy efficiency; both utilise the new technologies; both would strengthen the power of the consumer and lessen the power of the mass producer.

Invest in the future In every sphere, Citizens' Britain moves away from a wasteful squandering of resources on today's consumption and towards policies for future success. This theme is reflected in policies for education and training, in a preventive and holistic approach to health, in boosting research and development for industry, and in our plans for a safe and sustainable environment.

Think 'quality' Citizens' Britain shifts the emphasis from quantity to quality across a whole range of issues. Quality of product and design becomes the focus of manufacturing industry; quality of service and delivery the goal of our public agencies. In social relationships, as with ecological matters, promoting a higher quality of life becomes the dominant goal of public policy.

Enhance choice In Citizens' Britain, this means choices for all, not just the few who are rich enough to afford the full range of market options. It applies as much to community care – for people with disabilities and their carers – as it does to education or housing. It also applies to allowing everyone fair votes, so that there is real choice in a pluralistic political system. Finally, it applies to employment, where increased flexibility and income security give wider options and better access to many people.

Disperse power This applies across the board: more control by employers in their workplaces; more influence by consumers on the market-place; more power for patients in the health services; for clients in relation to professionals; for residents in their communities; for voters over governments. In Citizens' Britain information technology is used to disperse the power of knowledge, and not to concentrate it. Greater freedom of information, enhanced civil liberties and more open government all enable and empower the active citizen.

Value what is shared Instead of prizing only what can be privately owned, possessed and consumed, Citizens' Britain will also revalue what is public and common to all. This is most urgently relevant for the environment, where neglect and squalor have made too much of present day Britain into a shabby slum. It is also a vital issue for the infrastructure, which has become overstretched and accident prone (especially in the field of transport); for law and order, where much violence and vandalism reflects a decline in civic culture and mutual respect; and in the social services, which are coming to be perceived as only for the poor.

Promote Partnership This is the underlying theme of a network which works through common interests rather than competition and fear of failure. Thus in industry, government and enterprises plan together a broad investment and training strategy. In the field of the Welfare State, users, professionals and the public work together to provide services which are genuinely community-based. In international relations, ecological dangers and the need for a lasting peace require nation states to cooperate in finding and applying global solutions. Citizens' Britain favours negotiated agreements in industrial conflicts; it favours a partnership-based rather than client-based relationship between experts and lay people over health and community care; it prefers voluntary rather than statutory regulation. And it seeks the management of international conflicts and crises through international bodies.

Part Two
Linking Principles

7

Introduction

There is an environment favourable to a good life and an environment unfavourable . . . the State does not directly enforce morality . . . it establishes rights, defines duties and creates opportunity for a better life.

Sir Henry Jones – New Liberal Group

During my adult life I have worked in the armed services, in the diplomatic service, in industry and in local government. And, like so many people in Britain, I have not worked at all, suffering two extended periods of unemployment. Mine has not been an orthodox career, but it has given me a chance to gain insight into several very different aspects of our society and some knowledge of other societies, too.

Why did I enter politics? The answer is simple. I believe that Britain has lost its way as a political community and I want to do something about it. If things go on as they are, we are heading for a society which is divided and fractured, which is organised on authoritarian principles and which runs on an unstable mixture of greed and fear.

We have lost our sense of belonging to a purposeful association, of being members of a community with goals that can be shared by all. People protect themselves from endemic insecurity by a cult of private affluence; businesses pursue short-term gain; government neglects or despoils the shared environment. With the decline of the importance of a class base in politics, political parties have become rootless structures, hunting ceaselessly for where the vote lies, rather than founding their activities on a clear set of principles.

What we need next is a new political settlement, a new deal for all our citizens which sets out the terms of a better contract between the members of a society and their government. In this section I shall look at the five major elements in such a new settlement:–

* Citizenship – a new settlement of the terms of the basic contract which defines the citizens' relationship with government and with each other.

* Government – a redefinition of the role of the elected authorities which govern Britain.

* Constitution – a definition of what should be the extent and limits of state power, and the opportunities for voters' influence and choice in Citizens' Britain.

* Environment – A description of how, in Citizens' Britain, the environmental imperative influences policy, especially in the economic sphere.

* International Relations – an outline of a new role for Britain in the world, as part of a more co-operative and negotiated world order.

8

The Power of the Modern Citizen

Those self important fathers of their country Think they are above the people. Why they are nothing! The citizen is infinitely wiser.

Euripides

At the heart of the structures we need to create in Citizens Britain lies a new concept of citizenship itself. For me the interests and potential of the individual which are paramount in politics. None of us is self-sufficient. None of us lives outside society, independent of others. Most of the things that give our lives meaning and purpose, our rights, our roles and our relationships, stem from membership of society.

Citizenship defines this membership, giving us opportunities to participate in, contribute to and benefit from our association with each other and the State.

Under the Tories – Subjects, not Citizens

Under the Conservative administration of the 1980s, the emphasis has been on unrestrained individualism, consumption and private property. Public life has deteriorated, standards of behaviour have declined, and our shared environment has become at best down at heel and at worst downright dangerous. People are encouraged to prize chiefly what can be owned exclusively, hoarded, or displayed in their homes. Status depends on money and possessions. Private greed has been elevated to the status of a public virtue.

It is no coincidence that we see increasing violence, vandalism and pollution in the public sphere. This government undermines communal resources and makes only reluctant provision for the shared environment. Its exclusive concern with the commercial, the private and the domestic encourages many people to see what is public chiefly as somewhere to dump rubbish, or to behave drunkenly and loutishly.

In today's Britain, millions of people are shut out of any share in prosperity and denied the chance to improve their lot. They are trapped in poverty by a system which ties their income to the level of public assistance through a combination of the withdrawal of means-tested benefits and the imposition of income tax. The government says that it is against dependency, that it wants to 'target' help to the poor. Yet it is creating an underclass which is excluded from the incentives and opportunities of the economy and denied access to property, status and self respect.

This underclass comprises long term unemployed people, trapped by their low earning power, or by the high cost of travel to work, and few job vacancies; black and ethnic minority people, trapped by bad housing, by low paid jobs and by discrimination and prejudice; disabled people, trapped by lack of access to facilities for employment, leisure and cultural activities; women, trapped into caring, without support for elderly or disabled relatives; and many other groups whose needs and aspirations are invisible in our increasingly divided society.

Creating this kind of underclass is not just immoral, it is also dangerous. When young, fit and active people can see no legal means of getting a decent standard of living, when they are shunned and scapegoated by a smug majority, when they are harassed by officialdom in the name of a coercive government, and denounced by judgmental journalists, they turn, as we see happening today, to illegal means – to stealing, violence, drug abuse and cheating on the dole. They will resent and resist the authorities, the police and the politicians who make the rules. I do not condone this, nor do I excuse it. I merely note that it is so.

In a recent speech, Sir Michael Howard, commenting on the fact that 50 percent of the electorate do not vote in the US (which, in the UK would be high for all but a general election) described these as 'an underclass, alienated from, and preying upon society'. Similarly, when people with illnesses, disabilities or frailties get no help and support they become withdrawn, apathetic or depressed, to the point where they need to be looked after by the most expensive, institution based public services.

There is a paradox at the heart of the present government's vision of society. They proclaim the enterprise culture, yet their policies trap people in dependency. They promote adaption to change, yet they have created real fear of change amongst the most vulnerable. Above all, they claim to uphold freedom, yet they rely increasingly on coercion.

Instead of 'rolling back the frontiers of the state', the Conservatives have rolled over the safeguards which protect the citizen. That is why they have to spend more and more on social controls – on crime, on police, on prisons, on punishment, on officialdom, on surveillance. Instead of increased self reliance, we have alienation and despair, more social workers, psychiatrists and probation officers, all trying to limit the damage caused by the decline in community and solidarity.

And this process is accelerating as the problems escalate. The present government has found it impossible to break out of the perverse logic of its own doctrines. It can only prescribe more of the same. The structure of our society is under threat from the destructive forces released by government policies, just as our health and well-being are menaced by neglect and pollution of the physical environment. We are relentlessly moving, step by step, towards Citadel Britain.

The New Citizen

A new concept of citizenship, suitable for Citizens' Britain, cannot be forged from old, post war institutions, which rested on the employment patterns of the 1950s and 1960s, on a purely domestic role for women and on environmental shortsightedness. The new terms of citizenship must guarantee universal membership of our society. They must make sure that all citizens get the basic resources they need to develop their full potential, that all have opportunities and incentives to participate in the economy and in their communities, that none is excluded or trapped in a subordinate, passive or dependent role. There are many muddled ideas about the rights and responsibilities of the citizen; many of them, indeed, fostered by the present government's negative and authoritarian philosophy. Here is my definition of a new view of citizenship for our modern society. It comprises three elements: rights, entitlements and responsibilities.

RIGHTS Rights give us the basic freedoms, we need to be full citizens in a free society. There are three categories of rights.

Civil Rights – freedom of conscience, speech and association; also freedom of information and equal access to the process of the law.

Political Rights – the right to participate in free elections on the basis of a voting system in which the power of the vote is equal in the hands of every citizen; to hold government accountable; to have information freely available; and to participate in processes of decision making.

Economic Rights - the consumer's rights in the market-place; employee rights in the workplace (participation and profit sharing); and rights of access to employment and to ownership.

ENTITLEMENTS Entitlements give us the opportunities and resources we need to be valued and valuable members of society. Political theorists have been used to thinking of citizenship purely in terms of political and civil rights but the ingredients of citizenship are not just political – they are social too. Indeed, one of our problems has been that while citizens have (in theory) been politically free they have been socially imprisoned within the state bureaucracies which supply what the state decides, not what the citizen chooses.

The creation of a society in which there is individual choice and social justice requires a new mechanism for delivering welfare provision to the citizen. I believe that this will best be accomplished by attaching to each citizen an 'entitlement' which defines their rights of access to health, education, housing and welfare. This should be, as far as possible, disposable in the hands of the individual. The role of government will then become to fund the entitlement, assure distribution and regulate quality, but not necessarily to be a monopoly provider.

RESPONSIBILITIES Citizenship is not defined soley as a bundle of rights and entitlements. It also entails the acceptance of responsibility, a fact which has all too often been dodged by 'liberal' reformers.

In a free society, people cannot be compelled to act for the public good, except in an emergency (for example, through conscription in wartime). But this in no way reduces the necessity for those interested in freedom to face up to the problem of creating a structure which encourages responsiblity, rather than one which merely provides excuses for the lack of it.

Rights and responsibilities must be complementary. They should strengthen each other, not be traded off in some politicians' auction. An acceptance of obligations can strengthen people's understanding of their rights: the active practice of rights leads people to take on additional responsibilities. The way to get the best out of people in a free society is by relying on positive incentives, not legislative compulsion. Already we have ministers talking about work as an obligation of citizenship, and suggesting that poor people should be compulsorily conscripted into 'training' or low paid jobs. The idea of 'workfare' is only canvassed because members of our underclass have no proper incentives to work or save. The government is increasingly relying on confiscating or cutting their benefits to force them into the labour market. It is a tragic irony that in moving towards Citadel Britain we would be ushering in a style of compulsory work, just as the Soviet Union is struggling to move away from this.

So, outside acts which are defined as illegal under the law, the responsibilities which go with citizenship in a free society cannot be imposed, still less legislated for. Nevertheless, society cannot run effectively unless the responsibilities of the citizen are broadly understood and accepted. It is here that the notion of community is so important, for it is chiefly at the level of the local community that citizens can understand their role, recognise their responsibilities and exercise their power over government.

The Labour Party's 1989 policy review missed this essential point. It passed in one hurried leap from old fashioned socialist corporatism, to a kind of modern rootless consumerism. It lost altogether the importance of the community as the seedbed of democracy and the place where our rights and responsibilities are held in common.

Meanwhile, throughout the 1980s the government's attacks on (and even denial of) the existence of community have been one of the chief causes of that sense of rootlessness and repudiation of personal responsibility which shows itself as anti-social behaviour in every facet of our life, from litter strewn streets to violence on the football terraces.

A new deal for citizens will establish citizens' rights, define their social entitlements and clarify their responsibilites to each other. It will not discriminate between those who have huge incentives to earn and those who have none. It will include all our citizens in the benefits of progress and prosperity. This is the way to bring out their best contributions to our society.

9

The Functions of a Modern Constitution

No society is free unless it is governed by two interrelated principles: first that no power but only rights can be regarded as absolute, second that there are frontiers within which men should be inviolable.

Isaiah Berlin

Britain can fairly claim to have been one of the progenitors of the 'civil society' in the modern democratic world. British ideas about freedom and the rule of law have provided the guiding principles of democratic constitutions in many other countries. Yet, paradoxically, Britain's own unwritten constitution has allowed authoritarian centralised government to overrun the whole fabric of our nation in ways which are destroying pluralism and diversity and which now endanger the process of democracy itself. What is new about Mrs Thatcher is not that she is confiscating rights we previously had but that she is exploiting to the utmost the potential of a system which never formally protected fundamental rights and to which the notion of an established citizenship is alien. The British 'constitution' (David Steel used to deride it as 'not worth the paper it isn't written on') was always vulnerable to a prime minister who had no sense of history and placed no value on the importance of convention. Mrs Thatcher did not make a new departure she merely used the powers of the 'elective dictatorship' which previous prime ministers have been prepared to exploit only partially.

As she has pressed home her electoral advantage, she has created a state authority which is secretive, unaccountable and more centralised than in any other democracy. Claims of national security have been used and abused to protect the government and infringe civil liberties; the freedom of the press has been limited; broadcasting has been subjected to interference and pressure, and civil servants have been told to put loyalty to partisan policies above the public interest. Local government, professional bodies such as the teachers and doctors, and even the Church of England itself have all been attacked as subversive. Scotland and Wales have been subjected to a style of government from Westminster which treats them as if they were restless outposts of empire.

A New Constitution

Britain's unwritten constitution of conventions and undertakings has thus become dangerously neglected and overgrown by state power. It is time to spell out the checks and balances, the distribution of power between centre and locality, the rights of citizens in relation to the state, and of minorities in relation to majorities. In the words of Samuel Hamley, Bishop of St Asaph 'In this country, the individual subject . . . has nothing to do with the laws, but to obey them'. If Citizens' Britain is to be achieved, this must be changed.

The time has come to address ourselves all our constitutional deficiencies simultaneously, rather than being forced back in defence of our liberties, one by one. The need is for a new democratic settlement which commits Britain to participative, pluralistic, open government, and curtails authoritarianism, centralism and secrecy.

The rights of the subject should not depend upon the benevolence of the ruler, even if that ruler is disguised as an elected parliament. Basic rights and fundamental freedoms for each citizen, such as a fair and equally weighted vote, should be fixed and non-negotiable, the centre of the system and the source of its legitimacy.

A Statute of Rights

We need a domestic Statute of Rights to safeguard the individual liberty of the citizen. This should be the central keystone of our democracy. We also need to look at other ways in which the 'rule of law', which A V Dicey (author of *Introduction to the Law of the Constitution*) and others identified as the twin pillar (with the sovereignty of the Crown in Parliament) of the British Constitution, could be strengthened.

Freedom of Information

We need a Freedom of Information Act which defines the rights of the citizen to information in a free society. The suffocating blanket of secrecy which has surrounded our modern British governments (and none more so than the present one) makes a mockery of parliamentary accountability, reinforces the arrogance and power of the executive and diminishes the citizen.

A Human Rights Commission

We need a single powerful body able to safeguard the rights of the citizen, implement equal employment and bring prosecutions under anti discrimination legislation. A liberal society cannot countenance the systematic disadvantage of any of its members on any basis irrelevant to their ability, such as ethnic origin, sex or age. Such discrimination runs against liberal values; it also denies people the chance to reach their personal potential and undercuts the basis of common citizenship.

Parliamentary Reform

We need a parliament which is worthy of our democracy, not a misshapen parody of it, like the present one. I dare say my view is regarded by most of my colleagues as somewhat puritanical, but I do not see why MPs should have other jobs. Our loyalty should be exclusively to the country and those we represent and should not be distracted by any outside influence. By the same token, we need a parliament that operates on a basis which more nearly matches the nation we serve. The ridiculous hours of sitting (starting at 2.30 and ending at any time after 10 pm) destroy MPs' lives and health, make it difficult to be a parent and an MP (which, of course, chiefly discriminates against women MPs) and unbalance any decent rhythm of government. Among other reforms to Parliament, we must have a much more open system of information, more powerful select committees and a system of vetting executive appointments.

We also need to reform the basis of membership of the second chamber (the House of Lords). This cannot be considered a priority, since the Lords, these last ten years, has been more effective at challenging the government, more open to television and the scrutiny of the British public and has conducted its affairs much more in keeping with the traditional virtues of British democracy than the wretched bear garden in which I have to sit. Nevertheless, in a true democracy power should not be derived from inheritance or patronage. It should come exclusively from the ballot box.

Parliament needs to be taken by the scruff of the neck and substantially reformed so as to make it more open, more effective in decision making and much more in tune with the needs of modern democracy.

Fair Votes

Finally, but perhaps most important of all, we must find the way to enhance the individual's democratic scope and potency. We need a just system of elections which enlarges the voter's choice and represents his or her view and preference fairly. We need to revitalise democracy by bringing it closer to the citizen, with stronger and more responsive local government, with democratic community institutions and with the provision of greater opportunities for participation in the decisions which effect our lives.

10

The Role of a Modern Government

It is the purpose of the government to see that not only are the legitimate interests of the few protect but that the welfare and rights of the many are conserved.

Franklin D Roosevelt

Governments at all levels ought to have a role which is on the one hand positive and purposeful and on the other clearly defined and prescribed. It is not sufficient to define the role of government simply as an idle bystander, while the free market is allowed to run rampant, with the most powerful winning and the weakest going to the wall. But, by the same token, the days of the corporate state are over.

Enabling the individual The chief function of government in Citizens' Britain must be to enhance, enable and empower the individual. This requires a society based on social and economic justice. Government is the guarantor of that economic and social justice because it is the mechanism through which the community regulates itself, allocates resources and decides priorities.

Regulating the market There will also be occasions when the free market does not provide a sufficient supply of the commodities and services which society needs, but which are not economic to produce. In these circumstances, it is a proper function of government to arrange for the deficiency to be made good.

In the economic market place, the primary task of government is not to be a participant but to be an enabler and, especially, to be the regulator which ensures that the working of markets is not only free but also fair, open and honest. It is, for instance, the proper function of government to break up the distorting power of monopolies, to ensure competition and to enhance and preserve the power of the individual consumer against the power of the mass producer or the high pressure seller. Moreover, a belief in the power of the individual and in the virtue of fair competition requires that the priority will always be in favour of the small rather than the large in the market place. For instance, it must be right to provide incentives for demergers, for buy-outs, for small enterprises, for small investors and for the employee shareholder.

Partnering success Neither can government afford to neglect its responsibility for helping to construct an appropriate economic and industrial strategy. Britain desperately needs to get away from the obsession with short term profit, which has dominated the City in recent years, an obsession which has been shared and promoted by the Conservative government. We must start by making the longer term investments which will be essential to a healthy economic and industrial base in a high technology future.

A crucial part of this strategy will be the creation of an industrial system in which the qualities of creativity, initiative, and especially participation are encouraged. It is here that government has a role in promoting employee shareholders, co- operative production and industrial democracy. The added value economy requires the fullest use of the human skills and potential which have so often been wasted in the past.

Guaranteeing entitlements In the area of social policy, welfare and the delivery of personal services (such as health and education), government should operate first as an enabler and only in the last resort as a means of total support. Allowing individual choice has an important part to play in this – but only if the choice is freely available to all rather than conferred on the fortunate few. So, in this area, the prime function of government is not to act as a monopoly deliverer of services, still less to force everybody to accept what the state provides. It is to define and establish its citizens' social rights of entitlement, to guarantee standards and quality and to ensure distribution and access. When it comes to our basic needs and those of our children, the citizen is entitled to equality of treatment by government, regardless of wealth, personal circumstances, beliefs or ability.

Upholding equality The second equality which government has a duty to uphold is equality of opportunity. Government must vigorously attack the barriers to equal opportunities created by inherited inequalities, discrimination or structural disadvantage. We should not be afraid of positive action in favour of individuals, groups or geographical areas which are disadvantaged. But governments should be much more sceptical about seeking to manipulate the result in order to provide a spurious equality. In short, it should always be preferable for governments to seek equality of opportunity than to attempt to engineer equality of outcome.

Providing justice Government's third concern with equality should be to assure equal access to justice. This is the first right of the citizen. It is the role of the state to ensure that each has equal access to the law, something significantly lacking in Britain today.

Justice has a broader meaning, however, than simply fair treatment by the courts. Individuals have personal rights which government has a duty to protect and, from time to time, extend. These include the right to be consulted about decisions which affect their lives and to participate actively in the making of these decisions. It follows that government must ensure that the citizen has a right to know about the actions of government and about the detailed information it holds on each of us. All these are vital ingredients of a just society and are therefore a proper subject for the activity of government.

Improving quality Another task also falls within the purview of modern government – that of setting standards and improving quality. If the market is to be given more opportunity in, for instance, the delivery of personal services, government has a role in overseeing the standards of quality for this private delivery. Effective delivery of personal services will be better ensured by government defining minimum standards of entitlement and quality for each individual and then interfering as little as possible in the means by which these are delivered.

Different methods of ensuring standards will apply in different areas. In the industrial area, where unemployment has undermined the bargaining power of labour, action will have to be taken to limit the growing power of those who control capital so as to preserve and enhance improvements in wages and conditions at work which have been won over the last century and more. Governments will always have a role in establishing basic minimum standards of safety and fairness in the workplace, but it will be better to protect and improve on these by enhancing the power of individual workers than by strengthening the power of unions or by detailed legislation in Parliament.

Sharing power There is one other matter which is not a task but a duty of modern government – to ensure that the power it uses is the minimum necessary. Here, once again, the claims of community become so important, for it is at the community level that the views of theindividual will most often find best expression; it is here that true participation can take place and real partnership be effected; it is here that the essential social quality of men and women can find effective expression. Government in the modern age cannot be effective unless it recognises this within its structure and expresses it in the way in which it distributes power. Government must recognise that it is a sharer, not a monopoly holder of power. We must abandon the illusion that parliamentary sovereignty in a unitary state must mean that all power is centralised at the national level.

Preserving peace If the nation is made up of communities, it is itself part of a community too. Our membership of the international community of nations imposes on us an obligation to preserve peace, to maintain international law and to tackle catastrophe and depriva-tion. It is the state's duty to accept these obligations.

This then is a different vision of modern government. It is a vision which requires a positive role for government but rejects the pretence of omnipotence; in which government acts not to direct but to enable and empower; in which government is more a regulator and guaran-tor of quality than a universal support system; where government, rather than trying to engineer outcomes or providing preferences for the privileged, works to ensure equality of treatment, of justice, of freedom and of opportunity for all; in which power is not held at the centre but spread within a nation built of communities, which is itself, part of the community of nations.

11

The Fragile Shell

The more we get out of the world the less we leave, and in the long run we shall have to pay our debts at a time that may be very inconvenient for our own survival.

Norbert Wiener

So far as we know, the thin film of air, water and soil which covers the surface of the planet Earth contains all the life that there is in the universe. Nowhere more than 10 miles deep, this unique layer is known to science as the biosphere. Within it live many thousands of species of plant and animal and five billion members of the one species that has come to dominate all others – man. By the time today's youngest employee retires, our numbers will have doubled to ten billion, all of them dependent for their very lives on the health of the biosphere.

No responsible politician can ignore the fact that we are now degrading and destroying our environment to the point where its capacity to sustain life is being undermined. As our numbers grow, this trend will accelerate. Unless we reduce our impact on the environment, our survival and that of many other species is threatened.

We expect political leaders to undertake, as their first duty, the responsibility to be alert to threats to our national security and to offer strategies to meet and reduce these threats. It is now becoming clear that the threat to our security posed by environmental degradation is every bit as real and as serious as the more familiar threats of war or terrorism. We must respond accordingly.

Holes in the ozone layer or climatic change resulting from the greenhouse effect are not simply scientific curiosities. Nor are they tomorrow's problems. These and the many other environmental problems we face will affect the quality of life of every citizen of Britain immediately. They now affect the prospects for our children even more. If our children and their successors are to live decent lives, today's parents will have to learn to take responsibility for the biosphere.

It is our own actions which threaten the species. Ignorance, greed and short-sightedness are familiar human failings. Combined with the awesome capabilities of modern technology they are deadly. Our technology has brought with it many benefits, but it has also brought unforeseen costs. These unlooked for bills have been building up for many years. What we are now confronted with is the final demands, which must be paid.

There are some who, faced with the magnitude of our environmental problems, hide from the future and prefer to bury their heads in the sand. They wish to reject the modern world and its complexities and retreat into an illusory simplicity. They blame all our environmental ills on 'economic growth' or 'technology' and wish to abandon both. Their feelings are understandable, but their advice is a counsel of despair.

There are others, Mrs Thatcher among them, who have come to a belated recognition that the problems are real and pressing, but believe that they need do nothing to solve them; that left to itself the market will resolve all our environmental problems as costs increase to the point where people are no longer willing to bear them. The problem with this approach, which puts ideology ahead of analysis, is that we may reach that point (as we may have done already with the ozone layer) too late to prevent serious damage.

What both these approaches have in common is that they are 'do nothing' strategies. In the first case, because nothing can be done; in the latter case, because ideology rules out intervention in the operation of markets. What is missing from both approaches is the fundamental recognition that our economy and our ecology are interdependent, that the health of one requires the health of the other.

Without a successful economy the capital is not available to invest in a working water and sewage system or in pollution abatement technologies or in energy efficient homes and factories. Similarly, ecological failure, be it in the forests of Brazil or Malaysia or the grainlands of the USA and the USSR, will undermine the foundations of the economy. It is no accident that the worst environmental degradation is to be found where economies are weakest. The lesson here is clear. Economic failure means ecological failure.

If we are to preserve the fragile shell in which we live, we have to establish the interdependence of our economy and our ecology as the guiding principle of all public policy. This requires government to play a strong role, not in dictating to markets but in setting clear goals, standards and limits for markets to reach, and then letting them get on with the job.

12

Britain's Place in a Modern World

I sit on a man's back, choking him, and yet assure myself and others that I am very sorry for him and wish to ease his lot by any means possible, except getting off his back.

Tolstoy

Like individuals, nations are not self-sufficient. The world economy is built on interdependence. Britain, with its long tradition of free trade, pioneered the mutual advantage of this system. But now, increasingly, we have to recognise interdependence in facing environmental threats and in solving international problems such as terrorism and the spread of AIDs. And, even more fundamentally, in the nuclear age we will have to assure our peace less through opposing systems of collective defence and more through recognition of our mutual interests in common security.

Why is it that President Gorbachov, in his speech to the United Nations, emphasised all these benefits of co-operation between nations, whereas Mrs Thatcher always continues to sound both nationalistic and embattled? Why do all our partners in Europe socialist, liberal and conservative see advantages in closer political as well as economic ties, while she alone proclaims the virtues of separateness and absolute sovereignty? Why have we gained the reputation of being the dirtiest and most environmentally damaging nation in our section of the globe?

Economic development, the maintenance of peace and the achievement of a sustainable world environment in the future will all depend on a recognition that the importance of the nation state will decline while the value of international institutions will grow.

In the 1990s, successful advanced economies will become increasingly specialised in high-value-added, high technology manufacturing and in expert services, based on information systems. In an increasingly globalised economy they will necessarily depend on other economies to import components, semi-processed products, and lower-value-added manufactures; and they will rely on advanced partners for trade in finished products. Close political and economic links, such as those which will be facilitated by a more united Europe, will greatly assist the exchange of expert service and information on which development in the future will depend.

All the major West European nations face three major challenges in the 1990s. First, there is the continued rapid economic advance of the countries of the Pacific Basin. The next wave of growth and technological change is almost certain to be strongest in that part of the world. In order to make an effective response to industrial competition from the Pacific Basin, European nations must cooperate politically and administratively. If they do so, they will share in the benefits of the transformations that will accompany information systems and robot manufacturing. The alternative for Britain is to provide an assembly plant base for Japanese manufacturing penetration into Europe – necessarily a low value added, low wage base. This would be both politically foolish and economically short-sighted, condemning us to the status of a relatively low-productivity and backward economy.

Second, there is the changing nature of the Atlantic relationship. The move towards a more multi-sided world in which there are many more centres of power and the growth of a distinctive European identity will cause an increasing divergence of national interest between Europe and the United States. In particular, Europe will develop closer ties with Eastern Europe, while the US will have to respond to the new economicpowers of the Pacific. Managing this period of change in the Atlantic relationship will require great sensitivity if the forces of isolationism in the US and anti-Americanism in Europe are to be kept in check. Europe will have to find ways of carrying more of the burden of its own defence and to respond in a more co-ordinated fashion to world events.

Third, there are the remarkable changes taking place in the Soviet Union and Eastern Europe. These hold out enormous promise. But they also present considerable problems. The promise is of extensive trade opportunities and important changes in defence priorities. Unless there is political co-ordination in Western Europe, it is West

Germany, acting alone, that stands to gain most from these changes. If the rest of the European Community chooses to act as an economic opportunist in relation to Japan, and as a defence and foreign policy satellite of the United States, West Germany (good Community partner though she is) will be driven into an independent policy initiative with her Eastern neighbours. It would be impossible for West Germany to resist the political advantages – in terms of possible German reunification – as well as the potential gains for its efficient and proximate economy of this *ostpolitik*. The problems come from the tensions which will arise from what one expert calls the 'Ottomanisation' of the Soviet empire. As with the changing Atlantic relationship, it will take much skill and sensitivity to manage the pressures for greater independence in the nations of Eastern Europe without risking a potentially tragic destabilisation.

We will all have to recognise what the bottom line for the Soviet Union in this process is. I suspect that we will be able to go a long way towards the economic integration of Eastern Europe, provided we are prepared to leave the structure of the Warsaw Pact intact. I would not be surprised to see, in the next decade, Poland, Hungary and others established as associate members of the EEC, whilst still formally part of the Warsaw Pact.

At the same time as the East-West gap grows narrower, and bargaining, negotiating and agreement become more possible, the global North-South divide will continue to widen. We cannot continue to let the countries of Africa and South America decline into debt and destitution. We must recognise that our own environment and our health will suffer through such short- sightedness. If Western banks – for the sake of collecting interest payments on loans they should never have made – we force Brazilian farmers to burn out all the rain forests of the Amazon Basin, or Central African peasants to erode their land, then it is our children who will have to cope with the consequences of the greenhouse effect, and widespread famine and catastrophe.

Britain has an important part to play in world affairs, it will not be by narrow nationalism, still less by excessive pride in 'the British race', that this will be accomplished. International relations in the 1990s will require both a subtler and a broader vision. The big issues will need tact, a respect for other traditions, and an appreciation of mutual interests in co- operation. Flexibility, clear thinking and firmness, rather than an iron will, will be the qualities at a premium.

A truly strong nation does not need to wave its flag and brandish its fist at foreigners. Britain could have a less swaggering but more influential position in the world.

Britain's Place in Europe

Britain is part of Europe. We can either like it or dislike it, but in the late twentieth century we cannot change it.

I welcome it, and regard our membership of the emerging European economic and political entity as an exciting opportunity and a challenge. In discussing the title of this section, 'Britain's Place in Europe' a friend commented, 'That's a bit like talking of Hampshire's place in Britain.' He was right; Britain's role only makes sense as part of Europe.

The European Community's programme for 1992 transforms the whole relationship between European states more fundamentally than any event since the Treaty of Rome. This transformation is going to take place, whatever we do. We may, of course, try to delay and resist change. We might renege on our signature of the Single European Act and pull out. But we cannot keep things as they are. European unity will happen, with or without us.

There is a basic contradiction in Mrs Thatcher's position on Europe, as many members of her party recognise. She wants to have the benefits of European economic liberalisation without the social dimension of greater security and better public services for the Community's citizens, or the political dimension of participation in European decision making. But everyone else in the Community sees the three elements – economic liberalisation, social solidarity and political process – as a single package. What the Community represents – and therefore what we must join or not join – is something with *all* these elements, not just the ones Mrs Thatcher thinks are beneficial at the time.

So it is even more of a contradiction to insist on retaining full British sovereignty. If, we want the economic opportunities of the single market, we must bind ourselves to the political unit that creates the single market. After all, it cannot exist without a body with the pooled sovereignty to create it, so in the act of committing ourselves to the economic advantages of European free trade we necessarily bind ourselves to joint political decisions.

British industry recognises this. Increasingly I hear people in the business community puzzling about Mrs Thatcher's position and questioning her logic. They see that the economic opportunity is there but that it carries clear political and social implications. There is a paradox here. The British government has spent millions of pounds on a programme of public education for business about 1992. The result is that business people are now only too aware of the irrational and contradictory stance the government itself has taken in response to 1992.

The political transition to the new Europe will not be easy. I have argued that Britain faces a constitutional crisis over whether power will be centralised, secretive and unaccountable or dispersed, open and democratic. Europe faces a parallel crisis.

Because economic measures came before political development, the Community is, indeed run by a bureaucracy. This is not, as Mrs Thatcher claims, because Europe is excessively politicised. It is because it is not political enough – its economic institutions are not yet properly answerable to its elected representatives. The real issue of sovereignty in Europe, as in Britain, is how to make the executive properly accountable to the people, how to make Europe a political democracy,rather than an economic bureaucracy.

There is a constitutional turning point, perhaps even a crisis, coming in Europe. The question which must be answered is the age old one – who governs? Is it the Council of Ministers and the bureaucracy, or is it the elected representatives? I am confident that democracy will prevail, and that we in Britain have much to contribute, and much to gain, from a new political settlement which will give us all a new level of civil, political and social rights as European citizens, as well as British ones. Just as most of our European partners are more prosperous and more efficient than we are, so most of them have more democratic and open societies. And most give their citizens better social services. For those of us who have lost rather than gained in the British transformations of the 1980s, the European transformations of the 1990s are a refreshing and welcome prospect.

Part Three
Policy Areas

13

Personal Services

Introduction

Society is a kind of parent to its members. If it, and they, are to thrive, its values must be clear, coherent and generally acceptable.

Milton R Sapirstein

When I travel in Europe I am constantly struck by one vivid impression. In comparison with Britain, the public environment in many other European countries is excellent. Where ours looks shoddy, neglected, stressed and depleted, theirs is generally sparkling, clean, welcoming and generous. Our neighbours take a pride in their public services – and it shows.

It also shows in the way national resources are used to create a healthy and convivial local environment. Driving through small towns in France or Germany recently, I have been especially struck by the sports facilities – lavishly provided and beautifully maintained. It shows in the way public buildings are constructed, in the furniture, the equipment, the staff, the overall atmosphere. Visit a town hall or a clinic in the Netherlands and you can readily see the difference from Britain. There is a civic culture which values what is public and believes that citizens are entitled to respect and quality.

I am often ashamed that my country's civic culture has degenerated to such depths during my time in public life. I am embarrassed when foreign visitors walking round our capital city see young people sleeping in streets and under bridges, encounter beggars in the parks and alleys, witness squalor and decay on council housing estates. But these are just the outward signs of a declining quality of life for all our people. What doesn't show is much worse – the misery of child abuse, the scandal of youngsters driven to prostitution as the only means of survival, the loneliness and fear of old people shivering in unheated flats, the despair of carers, struggling to look after a severely disabled child.

The balance has tipped too far. Too much of our national wealth and income has been funnelled into private affluence – inflated house prices, extravagant imported luxuries – and into ostentatious, wasteful consumption. It is time to use resources to rebuild our public services, to revalue what we rely upon as the basis of our common culture.

In this chapter I want to take a hard look at our social welfare, health and education services.

Not all the problems we face are of the government's making. As we shall see, real dilemmas were pressing hard on the Welfare State long before the Conservatives took power. The government deserves some credit for asking some of the right questions, though very little for the answers it has provided. We need to find a new direction for social policy in the 1990s.

General Principles

Poverty, the grim tyrant of our races, abides with us through all ages and in all circumstances. For each victim that war and pestilence have slain, for each heart that they have racked with suffering, poverty has slain its millions.

Jean-Jacques Rousseau

Britain is rightly proud of the great institutions which were established in the first half of this century to serve, support and provide a civilised life for our people. The landmarks in the building of this structure provide some of the high points of twentieth century politics – Lloyd George's introduction of pensions in the 1906 Liberal Government, Rab Butler's 1944 Education Act and the Beveridge and Bevan plans for a Welfare State and a National Health Service.

These were the great corporate institutions serving a corporate state in a way which the rest of the world admired and copied. But the world is changing. Two factors now promise to transform these institutions in the modern age: the impending 'resource collision' and the possibilities opened up by the 'information revolution'.

First, the relative price of services is rising. As new technology transforms manufacturing industry, labour productivity increases, allowing production costs to be cut. We have already seen this happen, for example, in the falling prices of televisions, videos and home computers. Services, and especially personal services, on the other hand are labour-intensive, and productivity cannot be increased much, if at all. For instance, a hairdresser cannot cut more people's hair in a day now than he could fifty years ago, and not many more than a hundred years ago.

Yet as productivity in industry rises, so do wages; and although workers in service cannot match this increase, their wages tend to follow those of industrial workers. This is only fair, because it distributes the benefits of technology (which do not 'belong' to any individual or group) more widely in the economy. But it means that the price of services tends to rise in relation to that of manufactured goods. When this relative price effect is combined with changes in our population structure which produce a greater demand for health and personal social services, the result is a parallel increase in demand for our national resources, including labour power, to move into these services.

The second trend will have the effect of offsetting the first one. As more sophisticated technology, particularly information systems, become available to ordinary people, they can manage more and more of their daily tasks. Instead of relying on a bus, they can drive their own car; instead of sending clothes to a laundry, they can use a washing machine; instead of going to the music hall, they can watch television; and most recently, instead of going to college, they have been able to study through the Open University. In all these ways, the citizen can invest in equipment which makes him or her less reliant on the paid services of others.

We are on the threshold of a process which will transform the relationship between ordinary people and experts. With the advent of information technology, people can gain knowledge of subjects which were previously the exclusive province of professionals. This will not make the professions redundant – far from it – but it will change the nature of their jobs, from doing things *to* people to doing things *with* people. Instead of putting ourselves in the hands of experts such as doctors, teachers and social workers, we will turn to them for professional guidance about how to manage our own health, education and welfare, and this will fundamentally change the balance of power in the relationship between client and professional.

In the process, our opportunities for choice will be enormously enlarged. In Citizens' Britain we will demand that the experts treat us more as equals and as partners, that they share with us their knowledge, skill, and responsibility for the decisions which are taken about our lives. In return they will be released from many of the routine chores of their present jobs, and from much of the management work they now perform. This will transform the structure of the institutions which provide our personal services, making them less tied to buildings – hospitals, schools, offices – and more human, flexible and network based. It will also require changes in relations between professionals, leading to less hierarchy of status and control, more teamwork and communication.

All this will enable services to be far more cost effective and efficient. This is just as well, because the demand for personal services will rise considerably. The solution to this rising demand and relative prices does not lie, therefore, only in Conservative proposals for commercial style management and privatisation, but in giving consumers more power and responsibility for their own lives.

Yet there are many other aspects of need which cannot be dealt with in this way. In particular, a growth in the number of people aged 85 or more, and the better survival chances of people with severe disabilities, means that there will be an increase in the physical tasks of caring – helping people who cannot manage to move, dress, bathe or eat without assistance. Traditionally this work, whether it is low paid or unpaid, has fallen on women, and has either been done in large institutions or in the family home.

In Citizens' Britain all this will change. People with disabilities will not accept insitutional care. They will rightly demand independence and the chance to be full members of the community. Nor will they want the isolation and dependence of a purely domestic existence. They will want to have a public life, with access to communal facilities and to association with their fellow citizens.

Women will resist being treated merely as a reservoir for low paid menial work in institutions and a supply of full-time unpaid carers. As the demand for female labour in skilled occupations rises, so new ways of sharing the tasks of caring will have to be found.

The social services will have to find ways of supporting and supplementing the care given by family members – day centres, respite facilities and practical help. Instead of municipal services, rationed by bureaucrats, and delivered in standard portions (often not in the form or at the time required), Citizens' Britain will have support which is tailored for individual needs, sensitive to ethnic and cultural diversity, and flexible in its structure. There will be a wider range of services, more choice for consumers, and more influence on planning. Resources will be used to support co-operatives, both of people with disabilities and of carers. In the 1990s all these changes will transform the structure of our services and relations between providersand consumers.

However the basic founding principle upon which our welfare state is built must not change. This principle holds that we all collectively pay according to our ability, in order to enable us to have, free at the point of delivery, the basic personal services of which we have a need. This principle is rightly regarded as fundamental to a civilised society in the modern world.

It is this belief which causes so many to reject the attempts of the Conservative governments of the 1980s to slide Britain back to the bad old days, when paying for personal services at the point of delivery was a mechanism which blighted the lives and oppportunities of many and advantaged the few. The aim must not be to undermine the concept of the Welfare Society but to translate it into the modern age. Giving individuals a wider range of choice has an important part to play in this process.

But choice within a welfare system is not the same as consumerism in the market. The aim must be to provide choice for all, not just for the privileged or advantaged. This cannot be delivered simply by applying a raw free market system, where choice for some is entrapment for others. The impact of more choice will be limited and slow to develop. Improved choice can work effectively within a civilised welfare system only if it is properly informed. Indeed, providing information, advice and education to individuals about the opportunities open to them is an essential ingredient in any such system. The aim must be to allow the citizen to claim more power and control over his or her own life.

Here are some principles which should be applied to the development of state provided personal services in the modern world:

Funding people not instutitions Wherever possible we should seek to fund the individual, not the institution. The funding attached to an individual (their entitlement) should be as transferable as possible at his or her choice. Within the state system, the citizen's entitlements could be met either from a public or a private provider – but there can be no topping up (see below).

Entitlement Part of the enhanced status of citizenship should include a definition of entitlement to health, education, housing and welfare which is legally assured by the state on the basis of a minimum delivery for all. But, as far as practicable, it should be up to the individual to decide where and how this entitlement should be delivered. Suppliers of entitlement services, either public or private, must, however, be approved by the state.

Positive action No fair national system of provision of personal services can be achieved unless the government has the will and the ability to take positive action in favour of vulnerable or disadvantaged groups (for example the elderly, people with disabilities, residents of poor areas, ethnic minorities).

No monopolies The state should not enjoy a monopoly of provision in any of the personal services. Where separate systems for delivery outside the state system exist, however, they should pay the full costs of any staff, training and other services obtained from the state. And they must be subject to quality control by government.

No topping up Whilst any citizen should be free to leave the state system and ought to be able to expect good-quality provision outside it, there can be no question of them taking their funding with them. Any system which allowed topping up in order to obtain preferential treatment would be bound to end up with the poor subsidising the rich. The very mechanism to which we look to provide a civilised and coherent society would then become the instrument of division and widening disparity. The effect would not be just to recreate the injustices of the past but to reinforce them.

EDUCATION

Education is the key to ensuring that our future lies with Citizens' Britain, rather than Citadel Britain. A decent education is the essential prerequisite for the sort of flexible, egalitarian, mobile and open society which I seek. In an age when information, rather than heavy industry, will be the source of wealth, we cannot afford to lag behind our competitors in this area. But we are lagging behind.

More of our children leave school without qualifications than in any other major advanced economy. We have a lower proportion of young people in higher education than any similar society. And we have less pre-school education too. Even newly industrialised countries, such as Singapore and South Korea, are overtaking us in the race to prepare a well educated, adaptable and alert workforce for the age of information-based industry.

In Citadel Britain, minority dominance and government control depend on a wider population being kept ignorant and insecure. Citizens' Britain, on the other hand, relies on the widest possible dissemination of knowledge, not just for the sake of efficiency but also for democracy. Communities share skills and data as well as sentiments and loyalties; citizens have access to public policy and planning, and can contribute to a rational debate about progress.

In Britain today the education debate is in danger of splitting into two sterile opposing arguments: one holds that the state is the only effective and fair decision maker and provider; the other advocates what it calls 'market' solutions.

We are only too familiar with the limitations of the 'state-knows-best' camp. It has received such a battering in recent years that its case is hardly put outside the more backward looking sections of the Labour Party. For me, even if greater intervention by the state were desirable on educational grounds, this would be out weighed by its undemocratic and increasingly anti pluralist nature.

Strangely, 'market' solutions have not come under similar scrutiny, yet they have been used as a convenient cover for the government's moves for centralisation and more restrictive control. The imperfections of the market solution are many. Education is not a product in the way that hamburgers (or even council houses) are. For a start there is no clear product. Is it examination results? Is it HMI reports? Is good teaching a product or an input? These issues do not lend themselves to easy categorisation.

In reality, the educational market is as much about prestige, privilege and economic advantage as anything educational. That is why the clumsy attempts of the Conservatives to bias the system towards those with clout and resources are so utterly wrong and have been so rightly resisted.

There must now be room for an alternative vision of education which is based neither on an all-powerful state nor on confused notions of a free market. This is likely to be community based, democratically accountable, participative and responsive to changes in consumer demands, social and economic trends and professional advances. Here are some proposals:

Schools

Educational institutions should be independent, wherever practical. The government was right to build on the initiatives of Social and Liberal Democrat councillors in Cambridgeshire who pioneered systems to give schools the freedom to manage their own budgets, employ teachers and other staff and determine the balance of educational provisions, within common guidelines. Indeed, I have no objection to privately run schools serving the public sector provided they both submit to Local Education Authority (LEA) admissions policy and procedure and accept LEA quality control and inspection.

Education Entitlements

A system of education rights and entitlements should be built up for all parents, pupils and students. These should include the right to an education contract (see 'Choice', below), the right to be represented in all educational decisions, the right to have educational needs assessed and negotiated and the right to a certificate of achievement on leaving education.

Flexible Education

More education should take place in the community and away from the buildings of the institution. Compulsory education should not be held to mean compulsory attendance at the same location for five years. Teachers should be employed who wish to work in community settings. We should establish suitable career paths for those excellent teachers who are not interested in the role of institution head.

Choice

Individual pupils and students should be entitled to a series of educational contracts, which would set out their rights to credits of free education. These contracts would map out curricular paths for each individual student from the age of 14. Between 14 and 16, the contract would be drawn up between the school, the Local Education Authority and the parent. At 16, the contract should be negotiated between the student, the LEA and the providing institution. This could help us to overcome the widespread feeling that education is something which happens to people and free the system up so that it becomes a much more participative experience. Curriculum contracts should also set out rights of consultation and representation, of access to files and to procedures for making complaints or raising issues.

Schools should be empowered to buy in curricular and other services so as to be able to offer a choice of curricular paths to suit individual contracts. These bought in services could come from teachers' co-operatives specialising in certain subjects, from other schools, from local sixth form or higher education colleges, from the private sector, or even, in the case of training, from firms. However, any provider of services along these lines would have to be approved by the LEA and subject to their monitoring and quality control. The costs of these bought in services would be freely negotiated by the school. In practise, however, they would probably relate fairly closely to LEA unit costs, while the provider, in most cases, would be charging on a marginal cost basis.

The Role of the LEA

The role of the local authority should be to provide and fund the entitlement and assure equitable access for every citizen. Apart from this, the function of the LEA would be to monitor, advise, provide central resources, plan for population trends, and guarantee rights. The LEA would cease to be simply, or even exclusively, the provider and would, therefore, be a much more effective avenue for democratic accountability.

Examinations

The examination system should become much more flexible and less bound to age. Institutions like people to fit into neat categories of users. This makes things much easier for the institutions, but it can obstruct the development of individuals. The main way in which education has sought to do this is by age and this will become more marked through the adoption of national testing. We must look for ways in which the educational process can be removed from age-related activities so that it does become a lifelong process. One way would be through the splitting up of courses into modules, so that students embark upon a particular part of a course when they are ready to do so. In the longer term, we should cease to tie examinations to ages (the driving test, after all, is not) and instead tie them to the times when they would be most useful to the individual pupil.

Pre-School Education

The citizen's entitlement in education should include pre-school education for their children, available from the age of 2 ½. I would not wish to see this established on an exclusively public basis. In poorer areas of Britain it may be necessary to use the LEA to establish a formal structure of pre-school provision, but in other areas it will be better to assist and encourage the voluntary sector, always providing that this can ensure sufficient pre-school places of appropriate quality to assure the entitlement to all. Whenever possible pre-school provision, in the form of a nursery annexe, should be closely tied in, and preferably co-located with the local primary school. We should set basic standards of what should be achieved in pre-school education, but the way that those standards are achieved should be left as open as possible. This is one of those areas where allowing flexibility and a variety of approaches will reap dividends, as the Montessori system has shown. Indeed, we may be able to go even further. Recent research has indicated that children can benefit educationally from being read to by parents as early as 6 months old. There could be a case for giving each parent, as an entitlement, access to a nursery education adviser who can provide help for parents on how to play and relate to their child in the most educationally beneficial way from the very earliest age.

Training

Education and training should be brought together into a single cohesive framework in which all levels are credit based (including YTS). All training should lead to recognised qualifications and should be structured to ensure the maximum possible scope for 'cross over' at any age between the vocational and the academic. There should be a remissible training tax, to encourage industry to work with education and training establishments in training its own workers. There should also be an established right to one day a week release for all employees under 18 for education and training, at the employers' expense.

Higher Education

We should seek ways to bridge the binary divide (between polytechnics and universities) so as to create a much more unified higher education system, which allows freer movement for students across disciplines and specialisations.

Education in Deprived Areas

There is a case for trying 'special contract' schools in inner city and deprived areas. These could be sponsored, or even paid for by private funds, but only on the condition that they submit to LEA admission planning and monitoring. They should, in the main, be smaller schools, with built-in pastoral care resources and perhaps even boarding facilities.

Parents' Rights

Parents must be given enhanced rights in education, but these should be concerned less with administering schools and more with being involved in their children's education. All parents should have the right to attend the school and participate, with the teacher, in their children's learning; the right to pupil profiles on their children each term; the right to receive regular briefing on homework and the right to have access to a designated teacher whose duties include home school relationships.

Adult Education

We should encourage the development of distance learning through the use of the new technologies. Local area networks can provide curricular resources to small schools and even to the home in a way which was not possible previously. Distance learning through computers will also bring about a fundamental change in the importance and scope of adult learning. This area will be one of the most exciting in education in the future – provided, of course, that Britain is up with the developments and not, as usual, behind them. Every citizen should be entitled to a period of adult or further education to be taken at the time of his or her choice. This entitlement might first of all be set at a years education, based on distance learning costs. This funding would be the one exception which could be topped up by the citizen (or firms, insitutions, and so on) to enable more expensive adult education to be undertaken.

Private Education

I long for the day when every citizen in Britain has equal access to an equally high standard of education. This will not be brought about by destroying the freedom to choose, but by enhancing it. In the meantime, the educational resource in the private sector in Britain is both large and valuable. To destroy it would be an act of senseless vandalism. However, we cannot continue to allow this sector to be divided off from the rest of education in a way which damages both the cohesion of the nation and the deployment of scarce resources. Steps must therefore be taken to bring together the public and private sectors on the basis of shared resources and developing partnerships. The provisions for the buying in of resources outlined above will provide one route for this. In addition there should be a role for formal partnership and twinning arrangements between public and private schools. There may even be a case for encouraging some private schools to turn themselves into institutions similar to the *grands écoles* in France. The charitable status of private education should be reviewed and the provision of private school resources to the public sector in the locality should be recognised as one criterion by which charitable status could be judged.

HOUSING

A visitor to Britain would quickly see that we are a divided society. The contrast between the opulence of our most exclusive private housing and the squalor of our worst estates is one of the clearest examples of how perilously close we are to Citadel Britain today.

In the 1960s, Britain had the best housing stock in Europe in terms of dwellings per head of population, rooms per dwelling and facilities. We have thrown away that lead. First we poured resources into building shoddy, unconvivial and cheerless high-rise structures for the public sector. Then we syphoned off cash and credit for the benefit of home owners, and new building came to a virtual standstill. Now we have spiralling prices and skill shortages in construction.

The housing market is cruelly distorted in Britain. In an average life, through mortgage interest tax relief, a home owner receives about £15,000 in personal support from public funds. If other tax reliefs, such as capital gains and death duties, are included, most home owners effectively get their house free. So the better-off majority of our households have all the advantages of owning an appreciating asset, and the richest of these get the highest state subsidy. Meanwhile, those unable to buy their own houses pay the full cost of their housing, and in some areas actually subsidise local ratepayers as well.

In 1988, with house prices rising between five and seven times faster than the general rate of inflation, many house owners gained more from the housing market than the total amount of their year's earnings. In years of high house-price inflation, it would pay the owner of a run-down dwelling to stay at home and do up his house rather than go to work.

The present system pours money into the pockets of existing

owners in the form of credit and tax allowances, forcing up the price of housing and making owner occupation less and less accessible to whole groups in society. Others rush imprudently in, for fear of being permanently excluded and end up, as we see today, by making themselves homeless when they cannot meet rising mortgage repayments.

Other than means-tested housing benefit, tenants receive nothing. This has trapped them in the rented sector and, crucially, prevented mobility. It is also deeply unjust.

Other European countries build more houses, to better standards, and with better access for all their citizens. To achieve the same, we must find a satisfactory and fair way to encourage both the right kind of house building and the right kind of help for people who need houses.

The Conservative government claims to leave things to market forces, yet it has not had the courage to tackle the distortions of state housing subsidies. On the other hand, it has disowned any responsibility for decisions about what sort of houses should be built, and where. The result has been a bonanza for speculators and a growing planning crisis in the overcrowded south-east of England.

The Conservative priority has been to break up local authorities' dominance of the rented sector, but it is achieving this greater pluralism at the price of rising rents and rising homelessness. There is an urgent need to increase the stock of well constructed, reasonably priced houses in the hands of socially responsible landlords for that significant minority who want or need rented accommodation.

The management of public rented housing can also be improved. Councils must become less paternalistic and better at involving their tenants in improving the quality of life on their estates. This will not happen as long as councils are totally preoccupied with finding accommodation for homeless people, much of it wastefully in hostels,with tragic consequences for family life.

Financial support for citizens which goes towards the cost of housing must also be reviewed. The main priority must be to end the dualism and divisiveness of mortgage interest tax relief and housing benefit, and to discover a fair way of offering support to all citizens which does not distort the housing market, or trap them in poverty or run-down, overcrowded or temporary accommodation.

Here are some proposals for housing in Citizens' Britain.

The Rented Sector

A new institutional structure to finance a new building programme for the rented sector must be established. I am strongly in favour of partnership funding between the public and private sectors – indeed, my local South Somerset District Council has led the way in new partnership schemes of this sort. Whilst there is no case for banning council building projects, the vast majority of building for rent in the public sector should be done on a public-private partnership basis.

It is too soon to say whether the rapidly expanding housing associations are the right vehicles for this programme. So far, their good reputation as socially responsible landlords rests mainly on their small-scale and rather specialised focus on certain needs. Their management structure may become overstretched by the rapid increase in their responsibilities. Rather than add further to these, it may be better to create new organisations (or to encourage their emergence) with specific responsibility for financing construction for the rented sector.

Land Value Taxation

Unused development and derelict land should be taxed on the basis of development value in order to encourage the developer to develop, rather than to speculate. It makes no sense to have, as at present, a tax system that rewards speculation and penalises reclamation. New housing will constantly be too expensive for those who need it as long as developers can make huge speculative profits on land. During the two great periods of housebuilding in this country – the 1930s and the 1950s – land was relatively cheap, and development profits were held down. A land value taxation system has many other fiscal advantages, including the control of inflation. In order to bring such a system into effect, we should set up a new 'Domesday Book' – a full cadastral survey of land use throughout the UK. This would also be an invaluable resource of information for national decisions in environmental and agricultural issues.

Housing Allowance

In place of mortgage interest relief for those able to buy their houses, there should be a new system of universal housing allowance for all citizens, based on need. Every one of us should have a tax allowance or tax credit which we are free to use either to finance the purchase of a home or to subsidise the rent. To encourage home ownership without pushing up house prices there should be a once- for-all lump sum grant, which could be used at any period in a lifetime, either as a deposit on a house or to buy furniture and equipment.

Clearly, mortgage interest tax relief and housing benefits cannot be scrapped overnight. They will have to be phased out, probably by not indexing mortgage relief. The new allowances would then be introduced gradually so that people do not suffer from sudden changes in their incomes. But the priority must be to correct the excessive distortion which favours the rich, in order to concentrate more help on people with average and below-average incomes and those just entering the housing market.

Power to Tenants

We should provide real power for tenants. If council tenants have a statutory right to purchase, so should private tenants. If housing associations have the opportunity to purchase and manage Council housing stock, so should tenants' associations (this has been done very successfully in Westminster). Where housing remains in council ownership, tenants must be given the right and the encouragement to take over the administration of their estates, with maintenance and repair budgets placed under the control of tenants co-operatives, where these can be properly established.

HEALTH

We have every reason to be proud of our National Health Service. It is extremely cost-effective. Its main problem is that we spend a smaller proportion of our GDP on health provision than other similar nations. (6 per cent in Britain – an average of 9 per cent in other advanced countries). This must be corrected. However, while more money will go a long way to solving the NHS's problems at the moment, simply throwing money at the Health Service is not the solution. We are going to have to face up to a major resource collision as health costs continue to rise faster than inflation, expensive technological health solutions become more widespread and the number of elderly and dependent increases.

In Citizens' Britain we will need to find not just more money but also new ways to ensure the health of the nation in the future.

The Conservative government recently announced its plans to reform the Health Service. They are right to seek to provide a Health Service which is more responsive to individual needs but they are wrong to become ideologically obsessed with a model based on commercial management and theoretical administrative structures. The result will be severe damage to our unified, free health service. Meanwhile, many of the real issues are not even confronted.

The long-term key to unlocking new resources and controlling spending is a shift in the balance of health care. We are all capable of doing much more to look after our own health, given the right information, and back-up from the professionals. Information technology offers us the prospect of being able to monitor our general well-being, specific conditions, and our recovery from illness. Instead of the emphasis being focused on spectacular and expensive cures, it can be increasingly directed to measures of prevention.

Our National Health Service has, in effect, become a national sickness service. Insufficient emphasis on keeping people healthy means higher costs to cure them when they are sick. This twin profligacy, robbing people of their health and money at the same time, has to be stopped. The key lies in providing far more effective primary health care in communities. Early first line action on illness can often be relatively inexpensive to provide, will save more costly use of scarce resources later and, of course, will lead to healthier, longer and fuller lives as well.

A clear example of this can be seen in cancer screening, where money spent on an efficient system now can save lives and money later on. Nor does this apply only to the purely medical area. I suspect that Britain will pay a heavy price in years to come for introducing charges on eye and dental tests, each of which has caused the take-up rates for these kinds of preventive screening to drop by two-thirds in the last year.

Two other problems will also have to be faced. First, health depends heavily on factors which are not under the control of the health service. If we are to achieve effective health care within limited resources, we are going to have to recognise the impact on health of government action in other areas (such as food production, pollution control, transport and planning,). An effective policy for health depends on creating a healthy physical and social environment. Research shows time and again that people who live in poor housing and receive poor nutrition suffer higher rates of illness, and that unemployed people are especially vulnerable. So are those under special stress – for example, women caring for an elderly relative without sufficient support.

Second, we must not leave decision making and the efficient distribution of resources in the NHS to the professionals. They cannot be expected to be able to balance priorities between prevention and the various kinds of treatment where their interests are so directly involved. We need a system with greater accountability and public participation in the health service.

When demand for services is limitless, and supply of them is controlled by experts with an effective monopoly, distortions are bound to occur. The fair distribution of necessarily limited resources is too important to leave to the medical profession. We must accept that issues of priorities in health should involve democratically accountable resource managers and, above all, individual consumers of health care. We all have a responsibility both to look after our own health and to involve ourselves in public concern over the services which protect it.

Health policies have recently emerged near the top of the political agenda, but it is not enough that people should be anxious about the future of the NHS. We need to engage this concern in a structure of participation, both of self care and of accountability within the service.

Here are some proposals:

Primary Care

We need a much expanded first line of health care, relying on a substantial network of community nurses capable of providing early treatment, screening, surveillance, health promotion and education and acting as a filter to more expensively trained and resourced attention from GPs higher up the tree. This kind of health care also has the advantage of reaching people in their homes in a way which can frequently be more sympathetic than impersonal surgeries and hospitals. In several health authorities teams of nurses, social workers and others have shown that good community care – for elderly, disabled and mentally ill people – can co-operate very effectively with primary health care teams, giving an improved service and relieving those with medical skills of time consuming tasks. Adequate, accessible services for community care will not only support carers, but will also free resources for other aspects of health education and prevention.

Family Practitioners

Until now, general practitioners have been the linchpin of the primary care system. Whilst they will always have an essential and central role to play, more use must be made of nurse practitioners, health visitors,community nurses and the like, who can deal with many essential tasks of health maintenance, thereby saving the GPs' time for the diagnosis and treatment of illness. This should result in primary care being delivered more effectively, less expensively and with more time available to consider each patient's individual circumstances. We should develop the concept of the primary care team, based on the resource centre provided by the GP's surgery or health centre. These should provide a 'medical consultancy' service to patients, informing and advising them on their options and opportunities and helping them play a greater role in looking after their own health.

We are still in the very early stages of a potential revolution in health care. For centuries we have been willing subscribers to the myth that health is the preserve of the medical profession – that we can only stay healthy by following doctors orders, by submitting ourselves as passive patients to their ministration. In the past, this myth gave the doctors power and prestige. Now they too are its victims. Modern medicine has recognised the need to engage patients in their own care and treatment.

The old approach cannot be sustained. Unless we become active in maintaining our own health, there is no limit to the proportion of the nation's resources which will be consumed by medical science. But doctors cannot force responsibility onto patients. It is only through a more equal partnership between the medical expert and the patient that the role of doctors can be transformed to get best value from their skills under modern conditions. Information technology can facilitate this process. But we need a change in attitudes, too.

Some important questions about the structure of general practice must be answered. How can we organise the service so that doctors have the time and motivation to treat patients more with the complete person in mind rather than just providing a 'snap-shot' response to each new symptom? How can we enable them to be less like medical technicians and more like advisers or consultants, helping patients get the best service from the NHS? Should all GPs continue to be rewarded predominantly according to the numbers on their list? Or is there a case for introducing some salaried posts in areas of greatest need, such as inner cities and very isolated rural communities?

The other structural issue is how to promote choice for patients in the primary health sector. Primary health care teams should be permitted to obtain medical services from any approved service, and they should be free to place patients in the medical institution of the patient's choice.

Hospitals

The hospital sector is by far the most expensive and complex part of the NHS. The government is right to raise the issues of efficiency and accountability, but it is wrong to confine its reform of the management of hospitals to purely commercial principles. It is all very well to talk about internal markets, but in a situation of unlimited demand and strictly limited supply there is always going to be a danger that greater budgetary freedom for hospitals will simply drive up the price of hospital treatment across the board.

So far, all the professions who provide the hospital services have opposed the government's programme and defended the present structure. But it is easy to see how, in the long run, opportunities for competition and price setting might allow powerful professional interests to gain advantages, at the expense of patient care. I would like to see attention shifted towards the accountable localisation of the service. Hospitals do need more autonomy in order to be responsive to local needs and concerns. We should see a return to representative boards of management for hospitals, with statutory membership for local GPs and other members of the primary health sector. Efficiency and cost-effectiveness are not inconsistent with responsibility to a community.

As part of the move to give more power, responsibility and choice to patients, hospitals should place more emphasis on advice about the management of recovery and rehabilitation. They should provide more than treatment and nursing; they should be equally concerned with information and explanation. At present no profession takes responsibility for this, and patients often leave hospitals without the knowledge they require to recuperate successfully.

This is part of a wider problem in hospital services. Increasingly, hospitals are becoming like factories, whose productivity is measured in terms of bed through put, the number of operations per day, and the number of patients discharged per week. Little or no attention is given to the quality of life this output sustains, to possible suffering during the recovery period, or to unnecessary relapse or complications. What is more, the government's 'reforms' are likely to make this situation worse. As with primary care, hospital treatment will be better integrated, and skills better used, when more paramedical employees are used to help patients get the best value from treatment.

District Health Authorities

It is right that health authorities should continue to enjoy a virtual monopoly of provision from the public sector within their area. They should however, also be able to obtain health services from any source, including the private sector. A large element of DHA funding should continue to be based on per capita costing, with adjustments to take account of such factors as social deprivation. In order to ensure proper cost control and accountability, consultants contracts should in future be with the relevant DHA, not the Region. Mechanisms to permit health authorities to compete for patients and provide services to other health authorities, where this is practicable, could benefit the patient. This requires further investigation.

Private Health Organisations

In the long run, I do not see any disadvantage in allowing private health organisations to compete to provide health care, under the following conditions: if treating patients inside the state system, they must not receive any extra payments for services above those paid within the NHS (that is, no topping up); patients treated outside the state system must bear the full cost, with the organisation paying the economic costs of any services purchased from the public sector and the net cost of any staff trained at public expense; they must be non-profit making and they must be approved, with the service they provide being subject to quality control by the health authority.

Self Health Medicine

We are already seeing in Britain a growing interest in holistic medicine and in natural remedies. This is an encouraging sign that people are begining to take more control over their own health and seeking to be active partners in health provison. While there are dangers in faddism, the public is becoming more knowledgeable and discriminating, able to recognise what is of value and what is quackery. These new approaches to better health should be integrated with orthodox medicine as far as is possible so as to give a holistic service rather than a range of competing, mutually sceptical, incompatible alternatives. Many of these methods are relatively simple and inexpensive.

Here again we need a more informed public, empowered with knowledge and choice. Patients should not be 'protected' by the authorities from complementary medicine and natural remedies but allowed to educate themselves in the virtues of a number of approaches. Above all, we should recognise that not all medical problems require high-tech solutions, and that controlling stress and sustaining a healthy environment are as relevant as drugs and surgery. Health education, as part of the curriculum in every school, has a vital part to play in this.

Patients' Entitlements

Putting power in the hands of the patient is best done by establishing:

a clearly defined list of patients rights and entitlements, including the right to choose a GP and to change practises;

entitlement to full and freely available information about GPs and other medical services in the area;

entitlement to full information on one's personal medical condition and the options for treatment;

entitlement to hospital treatment within defined periods published on a regular basis by the health authority;

entitlement to maximum freedom of choice, subject to the above, in selecting the timing of hospital treatment;

the right to dignified treatment;

the right of access to personal medical files;

the right, within reasonable costs, to have your baby by methods of your own choosing and at home or in hospital, subject only to an overriding decision by a consultant where it is believed that life is threatened;

the right of access to a comprehensive complaints procedure, including a local ombudsman service with the power to require action to be taken by the medical professionals.

Community Health

We should all be entitled to live in a healthy environment, a harmonious community, with good leisure facilities and a decent infrastructure. We are also entitled to a safe working environment, with tolerable levels of stress. These entitlements cannot be delivered to each individual separately, as a claim against doctors, hospitals or health authorities. They have to be part of what is due to us as members of our communities, and what we try to achieve through the democratic process of politics, and our membership of voluntary organisations.

Health authorities can play a part in this, by making themselves more responsible and accountable to communities. In Exeter Health Authority, for instance, any community of any size can set up its own locality planning team, in which professionals, consumers and interested bodies can participate. These bodies consider all aspects of health, from safety at work to sports facilities. And Exeter is one area where they are reversing the trend and opening new cottage hospitals and local clinics in many districts, as a way of decentralising and returning health facilities to the people.

Health is part of the quality of life – the most important part. It is not just about avoiding serious illness but about being alert, vigorous and able to fulfil our potential. Staying fit and active is not a burdensome chore but a way of enjoying life to the full.

I make no apologies for my own enthusiasm for fitness. I still maintain the habits of exercise that I learnt in the Marines. I really believe that time spent on energetic pursuits improves my concentration and stamina in all my other work. And millions of people are benefiting from this growing awareness of self health in their daily lives.

BREAKING THE POVERTY TRAP

A Basic Income

We have come to accept that one of the hallmarks of a prosperous and civilised society is that it should be able to guarantee not only good education and good health care to its citizens but also an adequate system of financial support for those in need. This was what the Beveridge system for social security set out to do. That was founded on the idea that every able-bodied man of working age would have a full-time job, paying a wage sufficient to support a family, and that the vast majority of married women would be housewives without employment. This was the pattern of the old industrial society. In the new industrial age all this has changed. Fewer men have full-time jobs, most married women are employed (mostly part-time), wages are far more variable and the balance between the working and the retired has altered massively (see *Workers versus Pensioners* by Johnson, Conrad and Thompson for a graphic and disturbing description of this).

The National Insurance system cannot cope with this situation. It has reached the end of a noble life and is going to have to be replaced.

Meanwhile, piecemeal measures have been taken to shore up the social security system. Under this government, far more use has been made of 'targeted', means-tested benefits such as income support, family credit and housing benefit. Because they all involve filling in long and complex forms, they are confusing and put many people off. Others are too proud to claim benefits which they get only if they prove they are poor. Sometimes the rules are so complex that even staff do not understand them. The result is long delays and inefficiencies, with claimants frequently complaining that the system gets them into debt, or even makes them homeless.

In spite of much trumpeting about reforming the system, targeting has been a failure because it has only reached between 30 and 70 per cent of those in greatest need. Much worse than this, it traps people in poverty. A Low Pay Unit report published in May showed that the number of people caught in the poverty trap has risen sixfold to more than 600,000 in the last decade, with those on half average earnings (£69.10 per week) still facing marginal tax rates of 95 per cent. For those people, 34p in every extra pound earned goes on income tax, 46.2p is lost in family credit, and 14.9p is lost in housing benefit. The report went on to point out that for 45,000 low paid families, the 1989 budget meant an extra 2.6p, compared with a bonus of £4.35 per week for the average tax payer.

Our economy cannot afford to have large numbers of workers with no incentive to earn more, and none to save either. What is more, the present system cannot cope with part-time work, which is such a growing feature of our modern economy. For people on income support, part-time work is useless, because their earnings are confiscated. The wives of unemployed men face the same problem. And the tax system leads to most part-time jobs for married women being offered at very low wages (under 40 per week), in order to avoid paying tax and National Insurance contributions.

This government has proved that tinkering with the system makes it worse. What was once the pride of the civilised world has become a bureaucratic nightmare, complex and expensive to administer, failing the poor yet damaging the economy. The time has come for a radical new approach. Britain should start to move towards an entirely new structure which gives every citizen a non-withdrawable Basic Income, irrespective of work or marital status. This would guarantee each individual a tax-free sum. It would end discrimination against women and against part-time workers, ameliorate the poverty and unemployment traps, replace pensions and help prevent poverty rather than merely inventing new ways to relieve it.

It will probably never be possible to provide a Basic Income which is, in itself, sufficient to meet the essential living costs of those in work. For the old, however, Basic Income, replacing the old age pension and paid as of right to all retired citizens, irrespective of their contribution record throughout adult life, can and must be sufficient for subsistence.

To finance this approach, all social security benefits, tax reliefs and allowances would have to be brought together into a single system, replacing benefits such as income support, unemployment benefit, etc.

That an individual's right to income maintenance would be determined according to the principle of citizenship is a radical proposal, but one which is quite in keeping with the traditions of our system of personal provision in Britain. It merely involves bringing personal maintenance in line with our public health and education provision, which are already founded, at least in principle, on equal rights for every citizen. Nor is the principle of making a payment in respect of people's status, rather than their means, in any way new. It is, after all, the basic principle upon which both child benefit and the old age pension are paid. It is in a sense the dividend due to every citizen on his or her notional share in the common wealth of society.

A Basic Income scheme has many advantages.

*It is simple.

*It is equitable.

It removes all discrimination against married women in the tax and benefit systems. Like men, women would have a sum that provides a modest weekly income if they do unpaid work, or a tax credit if they are in employment.

*It defines a right and an automatic process for citizens who are poor, umemployed, married or single parents to have their income supplemented. This takes away both the stigma of claiming and the power of state officials.

*It removes the distinction between full-time and part-time work, giving everyone the same incentives to earn and save, and married couples much stronger incentives to share both paid and unpaid work.

Economists like Samuel Brittan of the *Financial Times* are right in believing that, far from encouraging dependency, the Citizens' Basic Income will stimulate the take-up of spare employment capacity, encourage enterprise and self-employment, and provide the flexibility required in a vigorous modern economy. Indeed, it may be the most effective way to 'formalise' the black economy, since there will no longer be any incentive for 'fiddling the social' while moonlighting on a job. Instead of harassing unemployed people or creating occupational therapy schemes disguised as training, we will be giving people incentives and opportunities to contribute to the economy.

Another advantage of the Basic Income system is that it is well targeted, because people with higher earnings automatically pay back more than the value of their basic income through tax. We have become accustomed to counting tax rates as the only evidence of fiscal rectitude, and turning a blind eye to tax allowances. The basic income principle will make the whole scheme transparent, so that people will see what they are getting from it as well as what they are paying into it.

A perfect Basic Income system, in which every adult receives enough for subsistence, would, however, require all other income to be taxed at an unacceptable level. So we have first to implement the principle of basic income rather than its perfect operation. Indeed, it may take several decades of growing prosperity to achieve a Basic Income system, but every step we take towards it will diminish dependency, liberate economic power in the hands of the citizen and cut back on the oppressive power of the state bureaucracies over peoples lives.

What is needed is a gradualist approach. In order to avoid sudden changes in incomes and incentives, a partial Basic Income could be introduced gradually replacing both tax allowances and many social security benefits. In this way, the dignity, opportunity and choice of our poorest citizens can be improved without undermining the security of other claimants or destroying long-established rights.

The major principle which should guide our short-term policies is that no measure should be inconsistent with our long-term goals. For example, tax credits, which my party has proposed for many years, would clearly be a step towards Basic Income. So would increases in the level of the basic pension and in child benefit. Experts such as Professor A B Atkinson are working on step-by-step schemes for introducing this new principle.

A partial Basic Income would provide a basis that people could use to gain education and training, and to retrain during their working lives. The present nonsensical provision for student grants and the various training allowances could be simplified, giving greater choice and flexibility in this area, which is so vital for our economic progress. We must also recognise that it will always be necessary to give some people extra benefits because of their additional living costs. Disabled people need a higher basic income because they have a higher cost of living, and because they need help with everyday tasks. A proper disablement income would include an element related to the cost of care, which could be used to choose between various kinds of services – day care, residential care, family care, or an independent living scheme.

I recognise that a Basic Income scheme would take a long time to establish, but the time to start is now. Britain will suffer in future if our employment market is not quickly freed from the rigidities imposed on it by our antiquated and dilapidated welfare structure.

Community Care

As I travel round the country, I am privileged to meet people from every part of our community and to hear some of their personal anxieties and dilemmas. There is nothing more poignant than to have my hand gripped by an elderly lady who has struggled to sustain her life alone in her terrace house or cottage and who confides her fears for the future. Who will look after her when she can no longer get out of her chair or get herself dressed? What will happen if she has a fall?

Equally moving are the accounts of devoted parents who have sacrificed their careers and social lives to bring up a disabled son or daughter and who must now consider the future, as they themselves grow old. How will he or she adjust to new situations and new carers? Should the change come now, or should they try to manage a little longer?

When most people think of community care, they picture a large Victorian institution closing down and discharging people with mental disabilities or illnesses into a bleak, indifferent outside world. This is the legacy of the past. As the Griffiths Report has identified, there is a massive cohort of people, many of them in middle or old age, who have been consigned to hospitals for most of their lives, and who now have a desperate need for homes, supports and activities in the community. These people must not become the victims of change, a lost generation, abandoned because the old ideas on care and treatment have become outmoded and discredited. Nor should they be thrust upon relatives, many of whom were first advised to let them enter hospital, and then prevented from keeping up their links of family affection.

There are also new and larger issues for the future, which will affect us all. The proportion of our population aged 85 and over is growing rapidly. Among this very elderly group many are in need of hour to hour assistance with ordinary living. Most of them do not want to enter residential care, yet they cannot cope without practical help.

In the past it was taken for granted that the only alternative to entering a home was for a daughter or daughter-in-law to take in her frail elderly relative, but that is no longer always a possibility. Women's roles have changed and so have their aspirations: 60 per cent of married women now have employment; they have far greater geographical mobility. And there is a demographic shift occurring too. It is estimated that today a typical couple in their eighties have 40 surviving female relatives of whom 14 are not employed. By the turn of the century the number of female relatives of such a couple will have fallen to 11, of whom only 3 will be unemployed.

Meanwhile, a higher proportion of people born with physical and mental disabilities are surviving longer, and they are, quite rightly, demanding a decent quality of life as members of the wider community. They want independence and choice, not the alternatives of hospital or isolation in a family home. Their aspirations also require resources. So what price fairness for our disabled citizens?

Caring is not something that requires an expert, but the work that many unpaid carers do is heavier and involves longer hours and greater risk of injury than most paid jobs. There are well over a million such full time carers in Britain, and the majority are women. As the population ages, so do the carers – surveys suggest that about two in five are over 60 themselves.

The need for care among old people usually follows a predictable course. First the old person cannot bath without help; then he (or she) cannot walk outdoors without help, then he cannot dress without help; then he cannot wash without help; and finally he cannot feed without help. It has been estimated that between 1981 and 2001 the number of people aged over 85 in our population will increase by 646,000, of whom 219,000 will be unable to bath without assistance, and 65,000 will be unable to get in and out of bed unaided. When we recognise that almost half of these extra very old people will be living alone, the additional need for caring becomes immediately apparent.

Here are some proposals for dealing with the problem.

Flexible Care At present some 4 or 5 per cent of the population over 65 years of age are in some form of institutional care – about 100,000 in local authority homes, 80,000 in NHS long-stay hospitals, and 60,000 in private (commercial) homes. New methods of care could change these proportions. Experiments have shown that more flexible 24-hour support for frail old people living alone or with relatives could reduce the number needing institutional care to half or less. These new methods would not necessarily be cheaper, but they need not be more expensive either. Their advantage lies in giving both old people and family carers a better quality of life.

Services These have developed in a period when local authorities were obsessed with the idea of planned, centralised, bureaucratic departments, delivering standardised rations of home help hours or meals on wheels, mainly to people living alone. This is changing, but not quickly enough. If we are to rise to the challenges of the 1990s, services must be transformed.

They must become more decentralised, responsive to local needs, and drawing on neighbourhood resources.

They must have local budgets, so that local managers and workers in the social services departments can work closely with voluntary and informal groups and other statutory agencies.

They must be accessible and responsive to the varying needs of individuals and families. This means having a flexible capacity to give help when and where it is needed (for example, in the evenings or at weekends), with a range of staff working on a part-time or short term contract basis, recruited from the neighbourhood.

They must treat family carers as partners, sharing information with them, planning care, offering practical assistance, regular breaks and a chance to unburden themselves of emotional stress.

They must develop a range of transport, day care, respite, relief and residential services, to give old people and their carers real choices and combinations of options, not the take-it-or-leave-it alternatives of isolated, unsupported family care or total institutional provision.

People with Disabilities

Young disabled people have some of the same needs as disabled elderly people – they too need practical help or supervision in the ordinary tasks of everyday life – but there is one very big difference. Old people become more dependent on others over time; young people with physical and mental disabilities have a growing need for autonomy and independence. Services for these people and their family carers have to take account of this, providing training, aids, and eventually housing and care assistance for young disabled people to live independently, either in groups or individually.

There are still far too many disabled people in hospitals. Even though the quality of life of children with learning difficulties has been transformed by better education and family support, too many still enter old style hospitals for respite care and in family crises. And for those with physical and mental disabilities there is still a terrible gap in provision when they leave school or college. We need more training, recreational and sporting facilities, and better access to the world of employment and sociability for these young people.

Professional Co-operation

This is improving slowly, but there is still a long way to go. In future, local teams of social workers, nurses, occupational therapists and educators should work closely with carers in regularly re-evaluating and adapting plans that allow the best quality of life and development of the potential of these citizens.

Mental health

It is at last being recognised that mental health is something that concerns us all. In any holistic approach to health, the way we cope with stress and emotional pressures is of central importance. About a quarter of the whole population consult their GPs over psychologically based symptoms every year. This is why primary health care teams need to to be supported by teams of workers who can advise about the management of everyday stress and give counselling over relationship problems.

We should not allow the appalling neglect of many of our discharged mental hospital patients make us mourn the passing of the Victorian asylum, or try to turn back the clock. There will, of course, always be some people who need nursing during an acute psychiatric crisis, and others who need to take time out from broken lives or hurtful relationships. But most treatment can be given in day clinics or ordinary hospitals, and the need for rest, quiet and a break can be provided by small hostels in ordinary neighbourhoods. Some health authorities – notably Exeter and Torbay – have shown how the transition from institutional to community mental health can be accomplished. This is the way forward.

Community Care and Citizenship

The most fundamental issue for the new age is how to provide a life for those groups of citizens with special needs which exclude them from life as full and active members of the community. In the past we have penalised this group and isolated them in many ways. Some we have locked up in remote, regimented asylums, hospitals or workhouses. Others we have disabled by designing an environment which is a no go area for those in wheelchairs, or who cannot see or hear. Above all else, we have condemned all those people, and those who care for them, to poverty.

We need new methods of care, new access to ordinary facilities, and new income provision, but we must not allow the benefits we give to those with special needs and their carers to trap them in passive and excluded roles. For example, benefits to disabled people should not be made conditional on being outside the labour market, and benefits for carers should not – like the present Invalid Care Allowance – require carers to give up their jobs and spend a fixed number of hours on unpaid care.

This is where the Basic Income principle has the potential to unlock current dilemmas. If every citizen had a weekly income guarantee of this kind, then the only question would be how to give a supplement to people with special needs which recognises the extra expenses associated with disabilities, and takes account of their disadvantages in the labour market. A Basic Income would give a disabled person income security; a supplement for care needs would give real choice over what kind of care he or she would prefer.

Finally, of course, a Basic Income for all adults would allow family members to share caring tasks rather than trap one person (usually a woman) in the role of full-time carer.

This change should be an urgent priority. In the 1990s women will be in great demand in the labour market, yet the need for family care will also be growing at an unprecedented rate. It is morally wrong to expect women to combine both these roles, or to force women to make stark choices between them. A mechanism for sharing both paid and unpaid work more fairly is essential. Basic income provides this mechanism because it gives men as well as women incentives to do part-time work.

Disabled people and carers are both becoming more politically conscious and more articulate in expressing their needs. I welcome this. It gives us hope that they will press for equality of citizenship, which should be their right in the new age.

14

The Environment

We call people environmentalists because they are moved to defend what we call the environment; but at the bottom, their action is actually a defence of the cosmos, not of the scenery.

Neil Evernden Natural Alien – Humankind and the Environment

During the past decade Britain has acquired the reputation of being the 'Dirty man of Europe'. This reputation is not wholly deserved. In many areas our environmental performance has been as good as, if not better than, that of our European neighbours – on nature conservation, for example. But our consistently negative approach to European initiatives, our inability to propose positive alternatives of our own and our irresponsible attitude on such issues as power station pollution have caused a great deal of frustration. Thus the image has persisted.

Mrs Thatcher's recent interest in the 'green' vote is wholly welcome. I do not doubt that she is genuinely keen to be seen to provide a political lead in tackling global environmental issues, but her high profile and vigorous posture will not remain credible for long if she fails to back up global rhetoric with equally determined domestic action. This she has so far failed to do.

Indeed, the picture is one of rapid deterioration in British environmental standards. The present government's proposals to abolish county structure plans without replacing them with another form of strategic planning and its nonsensical plans to privatise the national nature reserves will damage just those areas of environmental protection where Britain has previoulsy been strong. Our continued resistance to the proposed European Habitats Directive will compound this problem.

Furthermore, it is now becoming strikingly clear that the failure to provide adequate resources means that such positive steps as the legislation to control pesticides and the establishment of the unified pollution inspectorate have been crippled at birth. Our toxic waste disposal system remains ramshackle. Indeed, this government has actively encouraged a massive increase in toxic waste imports. In addition, our already serious problems with water standards are being made worse as the water industry is sold off and private profit once again comes before public health.

This is not a credible basis from which to make any bid for international leadership. Yet there are clear signs from the polls, in the rapidly growing membership of environmental bodies, in the rise of the green consumer and even in the growing responsiveness of the business community that the British public wants much more rigorous action on the environment.

Here are some ideas for what a seriously committed government could do.

Action Programme

Environmental problems cannot be tackled in isolation from each other, nor are all our problems equally urgent. We must tackle the problems together but we must also establish priorities. This could be done by publishing a rolling three-year action programme that would establish clear targets and priorities in each area and identify those issues requiring urgent budgetary or legislative action.

Government Performance Targets

Government must itself set an example. Each department should be required to publish an annual environmental performance target. Departmental spending plans should be reviewed for their environmental impact by the DoE just as they are renewed for their economic impact by the Treasury. The budget statement each year should contain a statement as to its anticipated environmental impact.

Recycling and Waste

We should adopt a strict 'polluter pays' principle on industrial effluent and gaseous discharges. There should be established and significant financial incentives for re-cycling, which take not only into account not only short-term economic calculations but also include long term environmental impact. One of the chief of the these could be a tax, paid jointly by the producer and the purchaser, on all containers which are non-returnable (one example of such a tax has been successfully implemented in Denmark).

Gross Domestic Product (GDP)

We take for granted the use of statistics such as GDP to measure the health and success of our economy. It is easy to forget that the first national statistics appeared only in 1941 and that the Treasury refused to allow the pioneer of these, Colin Clark, to have an adding machine to help him with his work!

However, measuring our success simply by measuring pluses or minuses on GDP is now proving a hopelessly inadequate, even damaging practise. It has been calculated that, if increasing GDP is the first economic priority, then the most public spirited action open to the ordinary citizen is to take his or her car onto the nearest motorway and involve it in the largest multiple-car pile up. Every one of the consequences of this, from motor repairs, through lawyers' fees and hospital charges even to undertakers' bills, will all be incorporated into GDP and used to show that the nation's economy is 'healthier'. Similarly (and probably equally damaging), some industrial activity which results in increases in GDP is also inflicting terrible damage on our environment. For instance, the faster a resource in used up, the scarcer it becomes, the higher the price and the greater the increase in GNP if more of it is used. This is scarcely a sensible way to measure progress when the conservation of resources and the creation of a sustainable system is a primary purpose of public policy.

Much work is now being done by people such as Herman Daly and Kenneth Boulding on new and saner economic models which monitor not just industrial and economic progress but human and environmental effect as well. Already a physical quality of life index (PQLI) is widely recognised and used in the Third World. I do not believe that any of these will 'replace' GDP, but they will provide alternative indicators which measure not just outputs but inputs as well and which can be taken, together with GDP, to provide a more rational judgement about how we are doing. We should be prepared to promote and apply these as and when they are perfected.

Energy Efficiency

Energy generation and conservation should be brought together in the same government department so that a comprehensive cost benefit analysis can be conducted, which includes the option of increasing energy efficiency, before any new generating capacity is constructed (the government's own figures indicate that investing the cost of a new nuclear power station in energy conservation would save four times more energy than the nuclear station would generate). No new nuclear powerstations should be built. There should be an increase in investment and research into renewable energy sources, though I do not believe that these will ever contribute more than a small proportion of our total energy needs.

Company Environmental Targets

All large manufacturing companies operating in the UK, whether publicly or privately owned, should be required by statute to publish annual environmental performance targets and to have the attainment of those targets independently audited. The environment is every bit as essential an asset to a company as its capital or machinery and should be treated equally professionally.

State of the Environment Report

We need to know what is really going on in our environment year by year so that we can set goals and monitor our progress towards achieving them. The DoE should make an annual State of the Environment report to Parliament so that everyone could see clearly how well we are doing at improving our environmental performance.

White Paper

The business community, local authorities, teachers and everyone else in our society needs to know what part they are expected to play in protecting Britain's environment. Despite being ten years in office, the 1980s Conservative government has yet to publish a formal and comprehensive statement of its policy towards the environment. The DoE should publish, as a matter of urgency, a comprehensive White Paper on the environment and conservation.

European Environmental Agency

The European Community is the only 'laboratory' in the world in which to develop the international political tools which we will need in the future to manage the biosphere. It is vitally important that we strengthen the European Community's role by creating a European Environmental Agency responsible for enforcing the agreements which EC countries have made.

Global Warming

We will almost certainly have to give serious thought to instituting a 'carbon tax' to discourage the burning of carbon based fuels – but this has to be done on an international basis.

Financial Incentives

Regulation will, of course, have a part to play in protecting and enhancing the environment. But I believe that, in general, regulation will be less effective than using the market to discourage actions which are damaging to the environment and reward those which protect it. Governments should be prepared to intervene strongly in the market with financial penalties for 'damaging' action and financial incentives for 'good' ones. One example of this approach is differential taxation on lead free petrol. Similarly, in the West German state of Baden Wurtenburg, raising the price of pesticides to farmers has led to a 50 per cent reduction in their use. In a free market system, it will always be preferable to follow this approach first and only intervene with regulations if it fails. These steps alone will not, of course, guarantee us a better environment, but they will set us off on the right path to achieving that goal.

15

Industry and the Economy

Is it not conceivable that values borrowed largely from economic development miss some important points? Could it not be that tomorrow's 'rationality' and 'reasonableness' are not about work and production, but about a different shape for human lives.

Ralph Dahrendorf

A NEW INDUSTRIAL AGE

Introduction

I bought my first computer in 1981. It changed completely the way I went about my work and structured my life. Since then I have been fascinated by computers and, especially, by the way they will change, quite as profoundly as the motor car, every aspect of our society, economy and daily lives. Above all, the new technologies will transform production, making it almost unrecognisable from one decade to the next. Professor Charles Handy tells of a visit to a Belgian sugar refinery, where 270 people worked in rather unpleasant conditions. When he went there again a year later it was run by shifts of 5 people in a carpeted control room, with maintenance teams on call.

In future, industrial success will not depend on muscle power or even on manual skills. It will depend on brains, knowledge and communication. Clever workers, making clever products or providing clever services, will add value to small quantities of raw materials. The really productive workers will be researchers, designers, data processors, trainers and scientists. They will handle information in communications networks, through a range of media, and in complex organisational structures, quite different from those of today's conventional office or factory.

As in every other sphere, the key to success in industry is going to be quality and flexibility, and this is where the new technologies come in. Flexible production enables firms to meet customers' needs more closely. It will not be long, for instance, before car manufacturers will offer customers the opportunity of having a car model produced exactly to the customer's specification (colour, upholstery, extras) and be able to assemble this as a 'one-off' on their production lines. And those production lines could be anywhere in the world.

Japan has already learnt this lesson. Increasingly, their industrial enterprises consist of a nerve centre based in Japan, where production is financed, planned, reviewed and adjusted, and where products are researched, designed and tested. But the actual process of making things increasingly goes on elsewhere – the heavy manufacturing in South Korea, the textile mills in Taiwan, and the car assembly plants in Britain. So the really high-technology, high-added-value activities take place in Japan, while the less skilled and hence less rewarding work goes on in Sunderland, Seoul or Derby.

There is nothing inevitable about Britain's industrial decline. We have a potentially creative workforce and ready markets for our products. Even our post war failures and the steady fall in our share of world markets need not set the pattern for the future. The scene is changing so fast that new opportunities keep arising. But we must confront the issue now to avoid past mistakes.

Here are some changes we are going to have to respond to.

Organisation

In future, enterprises will not consist of an elite corps of managers, a hierarchy of supervisors, and a mass of manual workers. The decline of labour-intensive production has led to the knowledge-based network organisation. There will be fewer employees but they will be better trained, informed and equipped. They will also be better qualified and more mobile.

New enterprises will be less hierarchical and will require every employee to show initiative and self-direction. Workers will not be confined to repetitive tasks. They will have the intelligent machinery and the information to plan, monitor and adjust their own work tasks. They will want responsibility, not orders. Such organisations will have to be run by persuasion and consent rather than authority and control.

Quality

Modern industry's success depends on quality of product, not mass output. To succeed, the whole workforce must be committed to doing high-quality work and to meeting customers' needs. Workers in teams, improving their own standards, developing expertise, and training for future progress, can create an ethos of quality, an attitude of excellence. Quality is not only relevant to the production of goods for the external market; it also applies to the internal running of a firm, where quality of transactions between departments is becoming, in many successful enterprises, an area attracting increasing attention. Quality is also a key watchword in the service industries, where new techniques of measuring a firm's success by establishing levels of customer satisfaction are being developed.

This can only come about if high standards are upheld throughout the firm, employees are respected for their contribution to new thinking as well as their specific skills, and new technology develops the abilities of the work-force rather than de-skills them. In the long run, computers and robots are effective only if those who use them are enchanced in their capacities to think and create, not reduced to machine minders.

Management

In the network enterprise, all workers will have management skills, and the old distinctions between managers and workers will become as dated as that between gentlemen and players. The skills at a premium will be leadership and communication, teaching and learning, flexibility and vision. If business is increasingly a matter of making added value through the use of information, then running a successful business will be more like running a team than a factory. It will require the ability to get the best out of specialists and professionals of all kinds, creating an atmosphere where quality is valued. It can be done; if the best British firms can do it, why are AVERAGE standards so low?

WHY HAVE WE FAILED?

Research and Development

We must learn the lessons of past failures if we are to succeed in the future. The first lesson is concerns research and development (R and D). Developing new products and producing them by new processes requires science to be harnessed to industry; the two are interdependent. Yet Britain has consistently spent a lower proportion of national income on civil R and D than almost any other advanced industrialised country. This is the depressing conclusion of a whole range of recent studies.

For example, the November 1988 report *Save British Science: Science Strategy for the 1990s* pointed out that despite our excellent record of theoretical research we are lagging behind in industrial R and D. Government investment in R and D has been predominantly for defence projects; as a proportion of GDP, civil R and D investment by government has fallen from 0.73 per cent in 1981 to a projected 0.59 per cent in1990. This is at a time when proportional spending in other countries has been rising, and it leaves us bottom of the league of scientists and engineers engaged in R and D per 10,000 in the labour force. The figure for Britain is 30, compared with 65 in the USA and 60 in Japan.

In *Technology and Economic Progress: Proceedings of Section F (Economics) of the British Association for the Advancement of Science, Belfast, 1987* , Pari Patel and Keith Pavitt show that Britain's rate of growth in industry financed R and D was only 1.08 per cent, compared with 10.8 per cent in Japan, 6.59 per cent in Sweden and 6.53 per cent in Belgium from 1967 to 1983. Our share of West European patenting in the United States similarly fell from a healthy 26.3 per cent in 1963 to 15.8 per cent in 1985, while that of West Germany rose from 33.9 to 42.2 per cent.

The PA Consulting Group's report *Manufacturing Resurgence; Reality or Myth?* concludes that recent increases in R and D expenditure have been too low to sustain the 'product revolution' required to face up to international competition. It notes that the growth of industrial production in all countries since 1970 is closely correlated with the growth of civil R and D, and that Britain and the USA are almost alone among the main industrial nations in having negative trade balances in high-technology products.

Higher and Further Education

The second major area of British failure is higher and further education. Here again Britain comes bottom of the league. Japan, the USA and Italy have almost 30 per cent of their young people in higher education, and France has about 25 per cent. Britain has about 10 per cent. We train far fewer scientists, engineers and technicians than our main industrial competitors. Of pupils leaving British schools 43 per cent have no qualifications. We are sixteenth in the OECD league table of young people in education after 16 years of age – above only Portugal and Greece. In Japan, 98 per cent of young people stay in education until 18 years of age. In Britain the figure is 33 per cent. As the NEDC report, *Performance and Competitive Success: Strengthening Competitiveness in the UK Electronics Industry* remarks, 'Levels of apprentice recruitment have also fallen sharply in the UK since the mid 1970s with the decline particularly marked in the engineering trades.'

Amateur Management

Linked with this failure to invest in education and training is our tradition of amateur management. In Japan and the USA about 85 per cent of top managers have degrees; in Britain about 25 per cent. In West Germany, the average age at which aspiring managers join their firms after training is 27; in Britain it is 22. American top companies give managers 5 days a year training; British companies give about one day.

Japanese companies expect managers to understand every aspect of the enterprise, and to be engaged in a continuous process of self-education and self-improvement. A few British companies are following suit. For example, one British bank, in the process of reorganisation, allowed its middle managers the equivalent of one day a week for retraining throughout a year. It is this kind of investment in the future that is needed to reach international standards of professionalism.

Soft Targets

The fourth source of weakness has been our industries' preference for soft targets. Notoriously, companies have concentrated on home markets or, better still, on captive markets such as the public sector. The NEDC report on the Electronics Industry quoted above provides a case study.Although the UK electronics market has grown faster than the world average, British companies lost considerable market share in the period 1976-86, declining from almost half home market sales to less than a third. Yet this was despite the fact that they concentrated on the domestic market, relying on it for more than half their sales. As a result, their share of world sales fell even more. The major British companies tended to concentrate on protected markets, such as government defence contracts, which left them ill equipped to compete in markets for consumer goods, especially abroad.

Technological Change

Finally in this dismal list of weaknesses comes failure to respond to technological change. As we have already seen, this failure stems from weaknesses in research, organisation and management, but also in the whole structure of our industries. For example, a recent report by David Gann of the University of Sussex, *New Technology, Employment and Operative Skills in Building Services*, argues that technological change in construction is rapid but that the casualisation of building employment makes it difficult to implement potential technical improvements. The government's proposals for training initiatives to meet skills shortages are untested, almost certainly inadequate, and have been introduced without proper preparation. In another article, Peter Senker gives the example of computer aided design as a new technology which engineering firms are having difficulties in applying because of insufficient management training, and advanced ceramic materials as a new technology in which British firms are falling behind through insufficient R and D.

Investing in the Future

These failures are not going to be corrected by government policy alone, but Government has a role in creating a strategy, linked with long term measures to create a new climate in British companies. Government also has major responsibilities for education, training, research and science, all vital elements of the supply side of the economy. Our programme for the new industrial age should focus on the need for strengthening the links between knowledge and performance, discovery and productivity, information and industry.

School Education We need more degree-qualified science teachers to replace the large number who are teaching subjects without proper qualifications. Science teaching must be made more attractive to able people.

Further and Higher Education We must raise the proportion of young people getting qualifications of all kinds, and especially in science and technology. This means investing in our universities and polytechnics. It also requires government to be a major participant in training programmes.

Research and Development As defence expenditure becomes a lower priority, we must shift the emphasis from military towards civil research. The proportion of GNP spent on R and D must rise and government must invest more itself as well as finding ways of inducing private industry to reinvest more of its profits. Cutting corporation tax has not had this effect.

Collaborative Research Academic and industrial research must be more closely linked. Scientists should be able to move easily between universities and companies in a variety of roles, without major career changes. Collaboration with European programmes of research, which hasbeen waning, must be revived and envigorated.

Employee Participation It is not just the brains of scientists that will turn British industry round; we must use the brains of the whole workforce. This requires a structural change, allowing employees to contribute ideas, to modify methods, to adapt processes, and to improve quality. It requires a far more democratic, consensual style of organisation and new industrial relations. The best of British industry shows that it is possible; government must take active steps to promote good practise.

HOW WE WILL SUCCEED

British industry has become almost conditioned to failure, and has adopted defensive tactics as its share of world markets has shrunk in one decade after another. Any improvement in industry's performance has largely been confined to a few individual firms and cannot be described, as Mrs Thatcher would have us believe, as a country-wide miracle. There is no hiding place from international competition, and the single European market will make this truth even more plain. We must have a strategy for success.

The outlines for a successful strategy can be discerned, and I have sketched most of them already.

First, there are the supply side measures to improve the quality and adaptability of our workforce, to ensure that we are doing the right kind of research, to collaborate with projects in Europe, to engage the brains and energies of our workers at every level of production, and to get our managers thinking and acting in positive, forward-looking and developmental ways.

Second, there is the production process itself – the new emphasis on quality, the involvement and motivation of all workers as self-monitoring, self-educating, self-skilling members of teams, committed to excellence in what they do.

Third, there is the structural factor – the evolution of patterns within enterprises which allows these processes to happen. Firms need to develop structures through which communications can be improved and the benefits of new production processes maximised. In fact, as Charles Handy has pointed out in his book *The Age of Unreason* it is probably misleading to talk in terms of structures. What organisations need nowadays is cultures, networks, teams and coalitions. In this sense, business has become more like politics (rather than, as we have been encouraged to believe in the 1980s, politics being more like business).

These new structures for business and enterprise are discussed later. Suffice it to say here that, in business as in politics, the network strategy is a more efficient and effective alternative to the conventional idea of a 'citadel' organisation based on an inflexible hierarchy in which power is concentrated.

Fourth, there is the need to create a culture for long-term investment. Britain's economy is notoriously obsessed with short-term gain at the expense of long term success – 'casino capitalism' as it has been aptly dubbed. Politicians, the City and industrialists have all taken the short-term approach. Mergers are prime examples in the financial world. The effect of 'merger mania' is to make every company anxious to show high short-term profits for fear of a takeover bid. Capital markets are 'increasingly influenced by short-term considerations', according to an Executive Director of the Bank of England. And, with rapid turnover of stocks by large investors, there is a discount on expensive long-term industrial projects.

The result of this pressure on companies is to discourage innovation and long-term planning of the kind which characterised the successful era of British industry – the early Victorian age. This starves the future by choking off investment in the essentials for a successful industrial strategy. It helps explain why so many British success stories are companies which have low capital requirements – in fields such as advertising, public relations, retailing and stockbroking. Conversely, in more capital-intensive sectors such as electronics, opportunities have to be forsaken because of the lack of long-term finance ready to invest in projects.

Other countries have a co-ordinated approach to overcome these problems. Instead of having to finance their development by expensive short-term borrowing, as British firms are often forced to do, companies in Germany benefit form a well established debt market making loans over 10 years or more. German banks have close connections with industry and will often take equity in companies. In Japan, long-term low-cost finance is provided by industrial lending banks and government agencies. Interest rates are kept low and investment capital is plentiful and cheap. In France, direct investment subsidies are given to encourage long-term projects.

The UK consistently invests less as a proportion of GDP than virtually any other advanced Western country. Economists have demonstrated the close correlation between rates of investment and rates of productivity growth. As Carrington and Edwards remark in their book *Financing Industrial Investment* 'the rule that economies which do not invest do not grow is . . . as close to an unalterable law as economists may have yet found'. High investment does not guarantee rapid growth but low investment does clearly inhibit growth.

The government must set the right context of macro-economic policy. It should create a new consensus for long-term investment by taking the initiative in a genuine dialogue with industry and investment institutions, by taking a lead in relation to public investment in infrastructure, by allowing public corporations to borrow on their own account, and by a whole series of specific measures aimed at a constructive partnership between public and private funds to promote far-sighted investment opportunities, both nationally and locally.

The aim should be investment and recovery, not merger and manipulation. We should reward those who invest to create wealth more and those who speculate and gamble with it less. If banks, insurance companies and pension funds accepted their responsibility to invest in the future, we should be well on the way to a strategy for success.

A NEW INDUSTRIAL PARTNERSHIP

Sir John Hoskyns was nearest to the mark when he described the progress, or rather lack of it, of the last few decades in Britain as 'a gigantic accidental strategy that had relegated Britain from number two position in the world to economic obscurity and the brink of tribal warfare in less than forty years'. As a description of the part played by government in the decline of Britain over the last fifty years that seems to me to be as good as any I have heard.

While our competitor nations in Europe, North America and even the Far East seem to have recognised that the maintenance of an effective partnership between government and those who create the nation's wealth is more important than chasing perfect solutions, Britain has been catapulted between opposite sides of the argument about the ideological limits of the free market and state planning. Indeed, industry in Britain, far from being cushioned from the political battle, has been the very field upon which the competing armies have drawn up their forces. In the same way, the framework within which industrial relations are conducted has been ruthlessly reshaped by each incoming government in order to satisfy their own supporters and ideology. Is it surprising that British industry's chief industrial problem for the last thirty years has been its own internal relations?

Similar ideological battles have taken place over education and training, the nationalised industries, economic theory indeed, practically every other area which is key to the industrial success of our nation. Other countries have enjoyed at least a degree of long-term continuity. In Britain the only continuity has been in conflict.

Mrs Thatcher, of course, has claimed to have changed all this, by creating a 'new realism' on the shop floor. But it is now becoming plain that the few years of relative industrial peace in the Thatcher era have been more a product of fear of unemployment than a result of a fundamental change of attitude.

Industrialists are fond of complaining that politicians aren't close enough to industry; the opposite seems to me to be the truth. Industrial conflict is planted at the very heart of our political parties themselves. The problem is not one of too wide a gap between industry and politics in Britain, but rather that our major parties have become client organisations for one or other side of the industrial divide. It is scarcely surprising, therefore, that the government of the day is unable to construct and carry out policies which are beneficial to industry as a whole, that their actions, however worthy, become inevitably and quickly subsumed into the general body of folklore of industrial battle.

Since the end of the so-called Butskellite consensus (which itself was far less of a consensus than we sometimes like to remember) the ideological divisions between the two major parties have widened from disagreement about what must be done in industry to conflict over the role of the government itself. We have moved from the indicative planning of the 1960s to the present theory of non-governmental intervention – from a total belief in the power of governments to a touching faith in the miraculous influence of the market place.

In both periods (and in the interim stopping points between them), Britain's industrial decline has continued unchecked and unabated. After ten years of this govenment we still have the highest interest rates, the highest inflation and biggest trade deficit amongst the advanced nations in Europe. Meanwhile, net investment is actually lower than in 1979, industrial production has only just gone above its level of ten years ago, and our share of world markets has dropped and continues to do so. Our wage rises are running ahead of inflation at a pace which now threatens to swamp the gains in productivity we achieved at such high costs in unemployment. What is more, government seems powerless to deal with the problem. The old moss-grown tombstones of British decline remain depressingly in place, however much the government's propaganda industry would have us believe otherwise.

So I cannot share the government's optimism about Britain's industrial future.

The government has limited itself to monetary instruments but it is faced with structural problems, many of them long-term ones. Because we cannot match our foreign competitors for quality in a broad range of sophisticated products, we import an increasing proportion of these goods. Not only in world markets, but also in our own, we are losing ground. The truth is that we are going to need an industrial strategy and the will to apply it if Britain is to remain a prosperous nation in the face of rapid technological change, the increasing globalisation of world markets and the pressures of social division, deprivation and poverty at home.

I know the criticism that will be levelled at all this: 'It has been tried before.' But it hasn't. An effective partnership between government and industry is yet to be created. In the past, governments have sought either to conquer, or wholly surrender themselves to market forces when they should have been seeking ways constructively to harness these forces. Previously Government has sought either to command or ignore – now it must find the way to lead.

The problem, as we have discovered all too clearly from previous attempts at industrial strategy, is that government and industry are two very different animals. Governments are naturally averse to taking risks; industry must take them to survive. Goverments seek equity; industry pursues only success. Governments are publicly accountable; industry is driven by profit. Governments have to choose singular methods to reach objectives; industry follows multiple paths. Governments are as short term as the next election; industry has to consider capital involvement over decades.

Given these contradictions and past governments' inabilities at handling them, it is scarcely surprising that previous attempts at industrial strategy have resulted in the concept itself becoming discredited. It is not that industry in Britain lacks the public spirit. Quite the contrary. We have a fine tradition of social responsibility in business, which stretches back to the nineteenth century Quakers.

Public buildings in Manchester and Liverpol and numerous education and charitable trusts bear witness to this just as the Local Enterprise Agency Movement and such organisations as Business in the Community are an expression of it today. And yet, when companies interface with government, they sometimes appear to be narrow, mean spirited and concerned only to fight their corner and grab what loot they can.

The reason is not hard to find. Past government attempts at intervention have been restrictive, awkward, inappropriate and, more often than not, just plain damaging and wrong. Add to this wild switches in policies when governments change and it is not surprising that industry's first reaction when the man from the DTI appears at the door is to assume that what is going to happen next will be unpleasant and to conclude that the best thing, therefore, is to grab what money they are offered and run.

This tradition is not confined, incidentally, to Labour or Heathite Conservative governments. It applies to so-called non-interventionist governments too. One only needs to think back to Sir Terence Beckett's 'bare knuckles' speech of a few years ago for one example. Another can be found in the fact that the financial targets of the present government's medium-term financial strategy are not so much targets as weapons, which in many cases have been used in ways have been very harmful to industry indeed. Government cannot stay out of industry. What it does has an inevitable effect on business. It has a role, and it must play it, as this government has discovered painfully enough over Westland, British Leyland, Plessey/GEC and others.

Only government can decide on the resources being put into education and training; control monopolies and ensure fair markets; regulate and stabilise the exchange rates, decide whether to go into the EMS or stay out of it; set up trading and tariff arrangements; invest in the infrastructure industry needs to succeed; decide the relative disposal of resources between social welfare and economic stimulation; create incentives for more investments; in short, make decisions about what is good for the nation as a whole and therefore good for each particular industry within it.

And, if that has been difficult in the past, it is about to become much more difficult in the future. There are very hard decisions indeed to be made in the next decade.

How will financial resources be apportioned, as between the

competing needs of social deprivation and the regeneration of our industrial base?

How do we decide between cushioning the decline between older industries and encouraging the new?

What, after the 'big bang', are those parts of our industrial structure which are so essential that they must remain in our hands if our economic destiny is not to pass to others?

How do we decide between the survival of individual British industries and the merits of creating a wider European industrial base?

What are the sectors we encourage and what do we do with those we turn our backs on?

Britain's survival as a prosperous nation with a strong industrial base and a cohesive social framework will depend on how we answer these questions. Can we trust the government – any government – to get the answers right? Past experience does not give much cause for optimism.

Making the right decisions will, in large measure, depend on finding the right way to make them. It seems to me that the Tory and Labour parties are partially right in the way that they approach this problem. Labour is right in insisting that the government has a role to play in mapping out the future. The Conservatives are right in insisting that governments are very bad at making commercial decisions and that industry, assisted by the markets, will always do the job better. What we need therefore, is a partnership in decision making between the two and a framework to make that happen.

This is not to say that government should relinquish its power to make the ultimate decisions and be accountable for them. What it can do, however, is test the validity of its ideas against the industrial realities. More important, by reaching agreed strategic objectives with industry it can create the consensus for action which is so obviously lacking at present and which will be so vital in making the difficult decisions ahead actually stick. There is no doubt that our competitor nations do this better than we do – chiefly through informal consultation networks which are both more powerful and less exclusive to one or other side of industry than ours. The class war in Britain has destroyed such broad based networks here. We will probably have to use something more institutional.

Fortunately, a structure already exists in that much-maligned andignored organisation, the National Economic Development

Office (NEDO). It is necessary here to say clearly here that there is no place for a return to the government planning of the 1960s and 1970s. What there is a place for, however, is a serious attempt between government and industry to set some broad, high-level, agreed strategic industrial aims for Great Britain Limited. These aims might include realistic targets for, for instance, increasing exports, decreasing unemployment, integrating with Europe, and encouraging certain sectors. Below this, specific government policy proposals and suggested courses of action should be discussed on a sectoral basis of the sort initially envisaged in, but never actually fulfilled by, the little Neddies.

At a different level, the partnership should be regional as well as sectoral. Quite the most powerful impetus to all modern British governments' illusions of omnipotence and infallibility has been the increasing centralisation of power in Britain. The regions of our country should be allowed much more scope to take their own decisions within the broad framework set by the government, and this applies to industrial policy as much as to anything else.

Whilst it is beyond the scope of this book to provide the precise details of such a framework, it is possible to point some of the characteristics which would be required:

* a higher level of consultation which is essentially strategic and does not involve itself in detail;

* a lower level which is sectoral and regional; a process which is iterative – neither government or industry can second-guess the market;

* an objective which seeks always to create a consensus that will carry through political change;

* and an overall determination to work always with the grain of the market, never against it.

It is also possible to map out the general shape of an industrial strategy. Its essentials (all incidentally identified in a recent NEDO study of industrial strategies in other European countries)would be:

* a systematic view of the structure of the economy without any attempt at formal qualitative planning;

* a basic, realistic view of long term industrial priorities;

* a high priority given to investment and human resources.

Success in creating such a partnership for the future would require three changes. First, politicians would have to get rid of the ludicrous but widely held view that ministers are required to pretend that they are infallible. I spoke to a German politician recently about the admirable level of research and development in the German economy and the success of their government policies in encouraging this. He told me that his government knew that two-thirds of all the money they put into research was wasted. A third goes to charlatans; a third goes to firms which would find it from other sources anyway; but a third goes to real research and that is what really matters. The rest is a price that they are prepared to pay.

Such a thing would be impossible in Britain. The admission that two-thirds of the money going into any government programme is wasted, would call forth cries of 'Resign' from all sides. We must change this. Politicians working in the industrial scene are little different from managers. They make decisions about the disposal of resources in order to maximise returns. Some of the decisions they make will inevitably be wrong and it would be healthier for society as a whole and for decision making in particular if ministers at the despatch box were able, and allowed by opposition parties, to say so.

However, whilst politicians can make decisions about policies and instruments, they should be very wary indeed about deciding on detailed investments. There can be no case for a return to the practise of 'picking winners'. Politicians just are not equipped to do this. Much better to leave these decisions to the banks and lending institutions. But government can encourage actions which it considers helpful by underpinning lending, as in the Business Expansion and Small Firms Guarantee Schemes. Indeed, the basic concept behind these schmes is one which is well worth applying in other areas (for example to encourage investment in high technology).

Secondly, we will need a change in the attitudes of industrialists, too. Of course industry must fight its corner, but it must also realise that it is the government's job to take a broader view. To be fair, many senior industrialists do recognise this, as people such as John Harvey Jones have shown. But there is much more that can be done to strengthen this trend.

Lastly, we will need some institutional changes. We should start with the Treasury. It is there that economic policy and financial management of the country rest, in so far as they rest anywhere. The Treasury, however, is not very good at economics, largely ignorant of industry and a disaster as an organisation for financial control. It is not set up to deal with interlinked issues of any complexity and seems incapable of taking any but the narrowest view of any proposed policy or action. I would like to see a much expanded role for the Department of Trade and Industry, modelled on the Japanese MITI.

One thing is certain. We can't go on as we are. Forty years of decline is about as much as Britain can stand. What is at risk now is not just our industrial future, but our social cohesion too. The task of climbing out of the swamp is too big for government or industry alone. But it is not too big for both combined, if we can find the right way to build the partnership to make it work.

A NEW INDUSTRIAL SETTLEMENT

In the early 1980s, I worked as a senior manager in a West-Country based, national firm. My job was to establish an effective system for employee participation and profit sharing. It was one of the most formative periods of my life and one of the most rewarding. Since then I have become convinced that the whole structure of Britain's industrial relations is out of date and must be changed.

For decades now, commentators have been writing and talking about the 'British disease'. In the long litany of the reasons for our failure one dismal ingredient stands out – Britain's appalling record of industrial relations. Britain's image abroad as a strife-torn economy, summed up for many in the Peter Sellars film *I'm All Right, Jack*, is only slowly fading, and may well be revived by this year's 'Summer of Discontent'. Already we are seeing a return to the divisions and some of the tactics that did so much damage during the disputes of the 1960s and 1970s, culminating in the infamous destruction of the winter of 1978-9. As I write, the railways are on strike, as are the docks and the local government employees. But some things have changed.

After ten years of industrial legislation, the trade unions are considerably changed: they are undoubtedly more democratic and responsive to their members, and they are obliged to act more responsibly in their approach to disputes. I suspect that this will be Mrs Thatcher's most enduring achievement and it is not one which I believe any sensible future government should seek to dismantle.

Yet the underlying facts remain unchanged. Relations at work and in industry remain trapped in old thinking and old practices. Despite the bitter battles of the early to mid 1980s, and a deliberate decision to target the power of the the trade unions as part of a strategy for improving the supply side of the economy, recent events suggest that our divided society is just as divided in the workplace as it is elsewhere.

Today's economic environment is a very different one from the classic industrial economy on which the assumptions of this old thinking were built. The requirement now is for flexibility and not for standardised working. Efficiency requires high individual motivation, based more on skill and high-quality production and less on the mobilisation of a mass workforce. And the entry of many women into the labour market, combined with changing lifestyles and expectations, has left the organisation of capital and labour looking unadventurous, discriminatory, conventional and old-fashioned.

We need now to forge a new industrial settlement to replace the uneasy, often hostile, and cumbersome relationship between labour and capital that has dominated British industry for so many years.

The most successful of our companies are now those which know how to involve and motivate their employees by ensuring that they have a real say in decision making. The example of the National Freight Corporation since its privatisation, when employees were able to purchase shares in their own company, contains lessons for all firms. Others too have accepted that it is essential for their success to involve employees at all levels in the firm.

As we move away from the habits and institutions of the collectivist state, more emphasis must be placed on individual rights within the workplace, as well as elsewhere. It should become an accepted part of an employee's rights that he or she is consulted and kept informed about decision making within the firm. Workers have their rights through their status as citizens, and not just because they are part of some greater collective, whether of capital or labour.

For the Conservatives, trade-union reform was essentially a negative exercise. What could they get away with to limit the influence of employees and their unions?

For me, there is a positive agenda to be put forward. What can be done to realise the potential and commitment of staff and employees to their work?

Greater participation is part of a growing consensus for change, stretching right across Europe and North America. The European Community is putting forward proposals in its Social Charter and many of the most go-ahead companies already have advanced the practise of involvement and participation. I do not believe that politicians should be too prescriptive about this (this is a danger to beware of in the European Social Charter). There are many different models open to different companies. As in so many other areas, flexibility will be the key. As we learn from experience, the lessons of that experience should be put into practise.

A greater emphasis on partnership at work is a necessary but probably insufficient response to changing economic circumstances. Participation is desirable but will not be enough. The key to the radical reshaping of our industrial relations lies not just in giving employees a share in the decision making at work, but also in giving them the right to share in the ownership of their jobs and in the profits they help to create.

Every employee in Britain should have a right of access to a profit sharing scheme, if they wish. There are many established and successful profit sharing schemes to choose from. Some enable profit sharing to develop into share ownership which has a double advantage. I have been particularly impressed by the success of Employee Share Option Programmes (ESOPs) in the United States and elsewhere, where employees develop a real stake in their company's success. In Citizens' Britain it will be as normal for workers to own a share in their jobs as for them to own a share in their houses. Indeed, the modern mixed economy will be seen to consist not just of a public sector and a private sector but also to include other, more diverse systems of ownership.

In some cases, the present situation where capital employs workers will be reversed, with workers employing capital and even hiring their own management. The most obvious version of this will be workers' co-operatives. Despite the bad name given to co-operatives by Tony Benn and others in the 1970s, there are a growing number of successful co-operatives in the market-place today. Co-operative ownership is probably applicable only to a relatively small number of firms, but they have a place in the modern mixed economy and ought to be encouraged.

In other cases, there will be an element of community ownership – a particularly good example of this is the Mondragon co-operatives in Spain, which combine both community and worker ownership elements. In Britain, community involvement in creating jobs and establishing businesses has been confined to organisations like Business in the Community and the local enterprise agency movement.

These are early and hopeful models of the kind of much more diverse systems of ownership and participation which will be a key element of an industrial base in which flexibility of employment and the value of human scale in work and social structures will be important.

EMPLOYMENT

Flexible jobs in a flexible world

In the 1980s the graph of unemployment in Britain has been like a switchback – first climbing steeply to new record heights, then levelling slowly, and finally plunging down propelled by statistical manipulation, training schemes, pressure on claimants, and the consumer spending boom.

My Yeovil constituency has experienced all the phases of this fairground ride. In the early 1980s it was the older unskilled workers many in our traditional glove and leather industries, who were the first to be 'shaken out' of employment. Indeed, in 1981, I was one of them. At that time, I remember going to our local Job Centre to look for work and feeling anger and horror at the number of youngsters straight from school who discovered that there was nothing for them. This experience and the job I finally got (as a youth worker with special responsibility for the young unemployed) left me with a searing impression of the corrosive effect of unemployment, especially on the young. Then in the mid 1980s came the protracted crisis at Westland, when even the most skilled engineers, technicians and designers feared for their jobs. Now we are back to hectic activity, new hypermarkets, offices and construction sites, and a long list of vacancies in the local newspaper.

But employment is not what it used to be. We have not gone back to a pattern of steady jobs for every breadwinner, apprenticeships for young people and expanding manufacturing work. And we never will. What we now have is a kaleidoscope of new small businesses, self-employment, short-term contract work, part-time employment and subcontracting. For the young the choice is often between a government training scheme or an awkward working shift in the local supermarket or fast food outlet.

The new watchword is 'flexibility'. For the young professional this means a personal computer, a Fax machine, two days a week spent working at home instead of the office, and a telephone conference facility. For the middle-aged executive it means stress and insecurity, but, as a counterbalance, there is the appealing prospect of a lump sum and early retirement as an alternative option. For the long-serving local authority employee it means the threat of privatisation, with its implications for pensions and employment security. For the manual worker it means frequent changes of employer, home and job and spells of self- employment in a bits-and-pieces labour market. It often also means the hassles of claiming means-tested benefits, and the delays and debts that follow. And for working mothers this in turn means changes in their patterns too, as they struggle to adjust their hours, their child-care arrangements and their travelling to work to fit in with their husbands' overtime, short time, redundancy or altered shift.

These changes are just the start of a more fundamental transformation of the 'employment society'. We have had to recognise that 'full employment', in the sense of full time paid work, providing an adequate family wage for every adult male, was one very untypical phase in our economic development, not the culmination of a grand march of progress. In the past, household members all combined various sorts of paid with unpaid work – occasional or seasonal employment, home-based handicraft, part-time labour and subsistence production. We are returning to a situation in which even the most highly skilled will not expect a job for life, and many people will have a portfolio of different activities and interests and will retrain several times during their working years.

This has advantages and disadvantages. At best, it could be a stimulus for bringing out more of the individual's potential, and giving better access to employment for previously under-used groups. At worst, it could be divisive, leading to privilege, affluence and choice for some, and fear, toil and entrapment for others. We must recognise the new employment patterns now, and redesign our economic and social institutions to encourage flexiblity and to give all our citizens the chance to make their full contribution to the economy.

The New Patterns

In today's Britain over 26 million people are in paid work, and these numbers have been growing. But of these only 17.3 million are in full-time employment, and that total has been falling for some time. Some estimates indicate that the number of full-time jobs will be less than half the total by the end of the century. Even among these, a growing proportion may not be long-term jobs, or pay a wage sufficient to cover a family's weekly bills and housing costs.

Manufacturing employment has been declining since the mid-1960s. This has partly been a result of our failure to compete in world markets, but partly also a result of the new industrial age. As we have seen, the successful enterprise of Citizens' Britain will have fewer workers, getting better paid for more responsible, self-monitored, quality-oriented, highly capital-intensive, skilled jobs. The number of workers in research, design and planning will rise, while those involved in manual and supervisory work will fall.

In an age when information is the major source of wealth, the growth sectors for employment will include science, technology, publishing, advertising, communications, computer software, creative arts, architecture, personal services and leisure. Jobs in banking, finance, insurance, accountancy and business services will continue to grow, as they have for the past several decades. So will 'people related' professions such as teaching, medicine, law, psychology and social work, which provide services directly to citizens.

The proportion of jobs requiring reasoning skills will rise, while those requiring purely manual skills will fall. Already manual workers make up only about half the workforce in Britain. The Warwick Institute for Employment Research suggests that of the 1.7 million new jobs to be created in Britain by 1995, 1 million will be professional jobs or the equivalent; meanwhile, information-based jobs will increase, and 400,000 manual jobs will have disappeared. So we need from 30 to 40 per cent of our young people in higher education before then, not 18 per cent as the government plans.

All this sounds optimistic, in the sense that it gives a picture of a steadily improving quality of employment, conditions and pay. But we are not looking here at full-time jobs, mainly in industry, commerce and the professional services. In the 1980s the main growth areas for employment have been retailing, convenience foods, leisure and miscellaneous services. These increasingly involve low-paid part-time work, taken by married women and young people, often doing unsocial hours, with little security, no holiday or severance pay, and no coverage for National Insurance benefits. There is every reason to believe that these sectors will continue to grow, as people consume more personal services and enjoy more leisure. But if the labour market is not to be the major source of unfairness in our society we must address ourselves to the gap between the pay, conditions and quality of work of the 'regulars', and those of the army of low-paid 'irregulars' and 'casuals' who serve others' affluent needs.

The danger is that having a decently paid full-time job is becoming, like having your own house or a pension, a form of property. In fact, a full-time job is becoming the asset which gives families access to other forms of property such as homes, shares and cars. Once someone in the household (usually the adult male member) gets such a job, he will hold on to it for the sake of security , using it to gain some flexibility (through part-time work, self-employment or early retirement) only in his late fifties or sixties. But his job makes it possible and financially worth while for other members to take part-time work for lower pay and with worse conditions. Not so for the household with no male breadwinner or where he can't get regular work, or an adequate wage; their household income is tied to the poverty line, set by means-tested benefits.

This is unfair in two ways. It is unfair that women and young people should face such disadvantages in the labour market compared with adult men, and that men should have so few incentives to share the privileges of their jobs with others. And it is unfair that the incomes and incentives of members of 'job poor' households should compare so unfavourably with those of 'job rich' households.

It is also inefficient. It means that men in the prime of life, when they have most energy and creativity to offer, cling to the security of their jobs. They stand to lose more by retraining, or making a career move, than they can gain. Their scope for flexibility only comes late in their working lives, when they may have less to offer. It also means that women have their potential contribution stifled. While men are pursuing their careers, too many women are being sidelined into child care and domesticity; they often return to employment for which they are overqualified and underpaid. The economy is losing out because women are treated as second class workers by most employers – with some shining exceptions, such as certain banks, which have proved that, with a commitment to support and training, women's careers can follow the same patterns as those of men. (The same is true, incidentally, of all employers in Sweden, with the same results.)

If the new pattern is to be flexibility, less full-time and more part-time work, we must – for the sake of fairness and efficiency – give part-time workers an element of job security and employment rights to prevent exploitation and to close the gap between them and full-time workers. Our institutions must encourage job sharing, not job hoarding, if the new industrial age is to usher in Citizens' Britain.

The Organisation of Work

One reason why employment patterns are changing is that commercial firms and public agencies are organising themselves in new ways. Increasingly the organisational structure will consist of three parts:

The first is a core of permanent staff – professionals, technicians and managers – with key knowledge and skills, high salaries and fringe benefits, company pensions and perks, company cars, and so on. This core staff will be small and shrinking.

The second is a periphery of contracted-out work – both manufacturing and services. This will include assembly, clerical and maintenance tasks, done by subcontractors, some of them in other countries.

The third is an outer fringe of part-timers and temporary workers, especially in the service sector, who can be hired and fired at short notice, work flexible hours, and can absorb the impact of changes in demand, from season to season, at different times of day, or with altered economic conditions.

Core staff will be working under high stress, because the organisation wants to get value for its investment in them. To relieve this stress they will be equipped with all the electronic wizardry – car phones, lap top computers, Fax machines – to turn their homes and vehicles into offices. They will also train and retrain frequently, at the firm's expense.

Contract workers will be paid by results. Many people who are now employed on a weekly wage or monthly salary will in future contract to supply specific goods or services for a fee. Subcontract firms will be smaller and more vulnerable than large companies, and individual consultants will operate in the market with even less protection.

Fringe workers will move rapidly between employments, sometimes taking two or more part-time jobs at a time. They will have to be versatile and adaptable, and will need to be able to change their habits and lifestyles from one week to the next. People in the same household working in this sector will have to adapt their family and social lives to the requirements of their work. This needs good co-operation and mutual support.

The overall shape of an economy like Britain's will depend on the proportions in these types of employment. In a world of international enterprises, the rich and successful communities will provide the headquarters for firms whose manufacturing, maintenance work, accounts, clerical functions and even typing are done abroad. In an age of information wealth, communications, research and design, as well as finance and insurance, will be the sources of high incomes. Our aim should be to ensure that Britain is at the core of the new industrial age, not on the periphery. We must provide the highly qualified staff for organisations, not just be the assembly and administration works for companies with their headquarters overseas.

We must also take steps to look after all these different kinds of workers, to support them in a good quality of life that will enable them to do high-quality work. These developments carry dangers for employees in all sectors. Young, highly paid professionals jeopardise their health and their emotional relationships through stress and burn-out; contract workers veer between overwork and slack periods, with corresponding variations in earnings; fringe workers are often exploited and impoverished. If employing organisations are going to be restructured in these ways, then we must adapt our other institutions – public, social, family and especially our welfare system – to take account of this.

Discrimination and Employment

If employment status is the biggest single factor in determining people's status in other spheres – income, housing, wealth – then it is vitally important to give equal opportunity and access to jobs. We know that this is not happening.

Women Women still get lower pay than men – a third less on average. They are still concentrated in certain occupations. Women provide two-thirds of our teachers, nurses and social workers, but only 9 per cent of our scientists, engineers and professional workers, and only 15 per cent of managers. Women form three-quarters of all clerical, catering and cleaning workers, but only 5 per cent of transport workers. About 45 per cent of all women workers are part time. In most organisations men fill most of the top posts and women most of the subordinate ones.

This cannot be explained in terms of women's 'natural' abilities or preferences. In other countries, and especially in the Scandinavian ones, women follow career patterns which are almost identical to men's and have proved themselves in a far wider range of responsible and demanding posts. In Eastern Europe women provide the majority of judges and other high professional positions.

Indeed, I have for some time believed that we may be seeing a fundamental shift in favour of women in the job market. In the era of the flexible job, the flexibility which women have long since learnt to adopt, passing in and out of periods of paid, part time and family work, will be at a premium. Men have much to learn from women in these techniques of adaption.

The key to change lies partly in improving women's access to promotion and training, partly in improving child care provision, and partly in ways of giving men more incentives and opportunities to share their jobs and domestic tasks. It also lies in changing employers' attitudes to women. Where they come to be recognised as essential, coworkers (as in many banks) their prospects have been transformed. We must continue to strengthen and enforce the laws against discrimination. We will also need measures to encourage women to return to work, such as workplace nurseries, job sharing and flexible hours.

Ethnic Minorities Black people and those of other ethnic minorities are disproportionately over-represented among the unemployed, the low-paid, the self-employed, and above all amongst those who are overqualified for the work they are doing. No wonder there is bitterness in black and Asian communities when they are consistently denied decent jobs and training yet harassed by benefit authorities into low-paid work or unpromising government training schemes.

There is a real danger that young black people in Britain will become cynical and disillusioned. The white population is happy to acclaim their achievements in sport and music, but often assumes that they have little contribution to make in other spheres. Like women, our ethnic minority citizens have an enormous economic potential, which will be released only when these forms of discrimination wither, not just through the agency of the law but through the positive attitudes and examples of society's leaders.

Disabled People People with disabilities are still largely excluded from the labour market by poorly designed work environments, lack of basic facilities, and the attitudes of employers and fellow workers. As disabled people gain greater autonomy and independence in their living arrangements they will rightly demand better access to paid work. Some local authorities are setting a good example in the employment of people with disabilities, and they in turn are proving what high quality employees they can be. More active measures to promote similar schemes should be pursued across a wider range of jobs.

The Way Forward

Basic Income For fringe workers and contract workers with variable earnings, the basic income will it provide a secure, regular income for basic needs. It will improve incentives for low-paid and part-time workers, because it is neither withdrawn nor taxed. It will therefore ease these workers out of the poverty trap and allow them to make a full contribution without penalty.

For workers in transition between employments, or retraining, it will provide a regular source of income and so encourage both mobility and adaptability, as well as flexibility.

For core workers it will discourage job hoarding and give incentives for job sharing. As the level of Basic Income rises, more regular full-time workers will have incentives to share their work privileges. This is especially important for the status of women in the new employment structures. By giving each person an independent income, the Basic Income will allow child care and unpaid domestic work to be shared more fairly, for example by both partners having part-time jobs when children are young. Women would be able negotiate the flexible arrangments that will be needed in many households from a position of greater equality.

Although discrimination must be tackled as a separate issue, a Basic Income will strengthen the rights of black people by giving them security against official harassment, and change the terms of benefits for people with disabilites so as to allow them to be employed without penalty.

The Basic Income will also protect the poor and vulnerable from the threat of 'forced' labour, by undermining the case for 'workfare'. It will lead to a fairer and more rational distribution of paid and unpaid work among the whole population.

It will also enable us to see retirement much less as a 'milestone' in people's working lives. This will be important in an era when the numbers leaving school are falling so rapidly that incentives will have to be found to encourage women into the labour market and encourage the elderly to continue some work after retirement in order to make good the deficiency. Indeed, the Basic Income will allow people to have the process of retirement much more in their own hands, by allowing a gradual transition out of the labour market at a speed comfortable to the citizen, rather than the sudden and often psychologically disruptive step into retirement which is the lot of so many today.

Finally, and perhaps most important of all, a Basic Income will provide a real stimulus for self-employment and enterprise in a way which not only increases personal economic freedom but also provides a more efficient take-up of potential work in neglected corners of the economy and job market.

Quality Training This is essential for flexibility and fairness, and for national success in the new industrial age. Indeed, as a recent CBI survey showed, lack of adequate skilled labour is now the chief factor holding back greater commercial success and profitability in Britain. Even in high-unemployment Merseyside, the CBI found one-third of all firms quoting this factor as their chief worry. There can be no greater indictment of the government than that they preside, at the same time, over a great sea of unemployment and an industry which is being held back because of a lack of skilled labour.

I have emphasised in this book my commitment to investing in the future. Higher and vocational education is one of the keys to economic success, and we cannot afford to neglect it. A well educated and trained workforce will be adaptable and ready to rise to the challenges of rapid change. A credit-based degree system and access to a proper structure for adult education and re-training will provide the means to achieve this.

Government must play a leading role, and devote adequate resources to, technical training, which will skill and reskill our workers. We have had a decade in which government money has been committed to schemes for low-quality occupational therapy, low skill training, and anything else that will bring down unemployment figures. Now we see a sudden shift to making industry responsible for organising training, but with no guarantees of quality. Experience from countries such as West Germany suggests that these processes need to be for more carefully planned and co-ordinated than these sudden lurches from one structure and programme to another can allow.

Fringe workers should not be excluded from training opportunities. Community education facilities, where necessary, based on distance learning, should provide a variety of access courses, allowing participants to mesh their hours of study with their work patterns. More open learning opportunities for a range of practical training (such as those mentioned in the last paragraph) should be available.

INFRASTRUCTURE

Our Common Investment and Our Common Wealth

Britain has been visited by a number of terrible tragedies in the last few years: the King's Cross fire, the Clapham and Purley rail crashes, the Bradford and Hillsborough football tragedies; the *Herald of Free Enterprise* disaster in Zeebrugge habour. In all of these tragedies, a terrible price has been paid in human lives for cost cutting, lack of maintenance, poor planning and, in some cases, a lack of commitment to safety.

Our infrastructural services are the arteries and nerves of our economic and social systems. Maintaining them in good working order is a precondition for other activities, not an optional extra.

Neglect of our infrastructure is also part of the systematic devaluing of what is public and shared. Indeed, a recent report to the US Congress by the Washington Economic Policy Institute has showed a clear correlation between public infrastructure investment and high productivity growth. Japan leads the Group of Seven in the field with a public investment programme amounting to 5.1% of GDP and a productivity growth rate of 3.3% per year, while the US trails with figures of 0.3% and 0.6% respectively. The same survey shows that a given increase in public infrastructure investment (including in human potential) stimulates four to seven times as much in private investment. And lack of such investment encourages low standards of public behaviour. Under the ideology of the present government, railways, buses, public spaces and civic amenities are regarded as less valuable than private enterprises and retailing outlets. In consequence people tend to behave worse in them than they do in their own homes and offices.

These policies are counterproductive. They are supposed to lead to greater efficiency, yet nothing can be less efficient than a traffic jam, which stops goods getting to market; a train derailment; a workforce delayed or injured; a consignment mislaid. Failure to invest in a decent infrastructure damages the economy as well as the community. A recent CBI survey put the price of transport congestion in our nation at £15 billion a year to British industry.

It is a tragedy that we have allowed this neglect to occur at a time when there were idle human and physical resources in Britain. Single prestige projects such as the Channel Tunnel are no substitute for good national networks.

Indeed, the Channel Tunnel illustrates very clearly what is wrong with the planning of our transport infrastructure today. Low investment by the government has prevented British Rail from taking the action necessary to improve our rail network and freight-handling facilities to cope with increased Channel Tunnel traffic. The result is likely to be yet another lost opportunity. It is essential that proper planning takes place now to ensure that the benefits the Tunnel will bring will reach out beyond the South-East to the other regions and nations of the UK, bringing with it employment opportunities and a better distribution of wealth creation.

A Balanced Transport System

The most visible sign of failure in recent transport policy is the congestion on our city roads, and especially in the capital. Journeys in and out of city centres have become a twice-daily nightmare. In

London, it is calculated that the average speed of traffic is slower today than it was in the era of the horse and carriage at the turn of the century. Yet every year more people take to cars, vans and lorries as their means of transport. We are going to have to consider radical, even draconian measures to limit the use of private vehicles in our inner cities. A comprehensive plan to solve inner city congestion will include establishing effective and cheap public mass transit systems, extensive exclusions for private vehicles and the implementation of road pricing, using electronic tags or other technical means which seperately charge private motorists in the inner city.

Meanwhile, the government's solution to the wider transport crisis in Britain is to go on building more roads and car parks, and this has been the main direction of policy. Yet the failure of this approach is vividly demonstrated by the M25. Before it was opened, experts were declaring it inadequate; within a year it had become the country's longest car park, and now there are urgent plans to widen it.

The government recently decided to invest £6 billion in improving our transport infrastructure, all of it on roads. Meanwhile, our rail network is dirty, inefficient, unreliable and suffering terribly from underinvestment. And yet rail transport is more efficient and less damaging to the environment (both in terms of land use and in terms of atmospheric damage). What Britain really needs is a major stimulus to the modernisation of our railway system to create a much more balanced transport system.

A Modern Infrastructure for a Modern Britain

There is an entirely new infrastructural network which is required for our future needs. To make Citizens' Britain possible, we must set up a national interactive broad-band computer communications cable network. It's rather a mouthful and hardly the stuff for politicans to get excited about. And that is the problem – for the new information revolution makes such a network, capable of reaching into every home, as much an essential part of the infrastructure of an advanced society as are the electricity grid and rail and road networks today.

That was was one of the less remarked upon conclusions of the Peacock report on broadcasting. Their view was reinforced by the Prime Minister's own Advisory Committee on Science and Technology (ACOST), and the National Economic Development Office underlined the point last year when it said that the creation of such a framework 'in the same time frame as other countries is of crucial imortance to the competitiveness of the UK'.

Yet Mr Alastair Macdonald, reporting for the DTI earlier this year, decided that the government should play no part in establishing this vital infrastructure. The whole thing should be left to the market – which means, of course that it won't happen, because the market in Mrs Thatcher's Britain is driven by the same short-term view as her government itself. Mr Macdonald's logic would doubtless have also caused him to turn down the creation of an electric grid earlier this century, if we had been unfortunate enough then to have had a government which paid such exclusive regard to short-term profit at the expense of the nation's long-term need. Britain will play a very high price for such myopia.

The pity of it is that it would not be necessary for a government to provide the whole or even the major part of the estimated £20 billion required for a national interactive network to make it happen. Like the Channnel Tunnel, the government needed only to pump-prime the process and establish the framework. The money would then have been invested quickly enough from the private sector. As British Telecom themselves put it in a heartfelt, almost desperate, plea, 'All we want is some sort of horizon from the government, so we are not planning against total uncertainty'.

Meanwhile, the French, the Germans, the Americans and, of course theJapanese are cabling up as fast as they can – and, equally predictably, using a British invention (the fibre optic cable) to do it. It is fibre optics, in which Britain still has a lead thanks to the pioneering work done at BT's laboratories at Martlesham, which have made all this possible. The advantage of the fibre optic cable over its copper predecessor lies in speed and capacity. Already a fibre optic cable can carry information at a rate 140 million bits per second. By the end of the century this rate is expected to rise to 2,000 million Bps, sufficient to replace hundreds or even thousands of its copper equivalents. Fibre optic installation looks likely to be cheaper too. A US report calculates that the installation of a fibre optic cable to a new house is currently, at around $800, $4 or so more expensive than its conventional equivalent, but, by 1991, this will have been reversed, giving the fibre optic equivalent a 10 per cent saving over its conventional rival.

Up to now, the impact of the information explosion has been felt chiefly by industry. The coming revolution will be felt in the way we live our lives, organise the citizen's personal services and structure our society. A recent Dutch study has concluded that the commercial drive for such a system will not come, as our government all too typically predicted, from entertainment, but from education. With interactive curricular services capable of being delivered into every home and a desperate need for an adult education system capable of keeping personal skills and abilities up to date with the pace of technological change, there is a huge potential market here. Similarly, new ways of delivering health care, new opportunities for participation in the process of our democracy, new dimensions in access to information, new patterns of shopping and interactive entertainment will all become a part of our lives – or at least they could have been if only we had made the investment.

Britain is not just losing an opportunity to be a modern, information based society – it is losing a commercial opportunity, too, and one which we are uniquely well placed to take advantage of. It is not just that such a network will provide a much needed stimulus to our nation's still far too diminutive small business sector. Perhaps more important are the opportunities offered by the English language itself, for information is the world's new industrial commodity and most of it is passed around in English.

There is an interesting parallel here our Victorian forebears founded their industrial revolution on providing the rail, canal and road infrastructure capable of moving around their industrial commodities efficiently. They also set up commmodity markets to provide assured access to the raw materials they needed. And, in the process, the City of London became the commodity and banking centre of the world.

Information is industry's new raw material. The establishment of a national fibre optic network will be the means of passing it around efficiently. The establishment of national data bases containing all the information available and collectable, could provide the commodity market we need and an opportunity to add information brokerage to banking, insurance and the old commodities, as one of the invisibles by which the City earns its wealth. I have a strong suspicion that the merchant adventurers of the future will not tramp the world for commercial opportunities, but sit at home and trawl data bases for them instead.

Again, I do not call for the government to pay for this – the market will do that quickly enough if only the framework, the standards and the computer interfaces within which private industry can work are created.

On all this, it appears, we have now turned our back. 1988 ended with the government saying it was just not interested. Ironically 1989 opened with the launch of satellite TV. For Britain, it seems,the new age of telecommunications is to be confined to giving even greater opportunites for Mr Murdoch to come into our sitting rooms with his pre-canned soap operas, chat shows and opinions. We had the opportunity to give our citizens new powers to shape their own lives. Instead we have given new opportunities to the powerful to shape our lives for us.

This is a terrible waste. The network we could create for the twenty first century would be the basis for an active, reflective, democratic community, not a passive mass of mindless consumers. In Citizens' Britain, we could even create the possibility of direct democracy, with a well informed public telling the government its views on a range of issues of common interest, through the medium of such a system.

The trend since the age of city states and small republics has been away from the form of democracy in which the citizens gathered to debate and vote on particular and immediate issues, and towards the periodic election of representatives. The sheer size of nation states led to a democratic system in which the people participated only indirectly and occasionally. New technology means this is no longer a brute constraint – we can choose to combine direct and indirect systems of democratic decision making. This is the reason why those who favour Citadel Britain fear information systems, and seek to use them to concentrate control in the hands of the powerful few. Citizens' Britain uses them to spread knowledge and power throughout society.

SHARES AND OWNERSHIP

A Citizen's Stake in the Economy

One of Mrs Thatcher's proudest boasts is that she has encouraged much wider share ownership and created a form of 'people's capitalism'. She is right to be proud of this achievement, as far as it has gone. Yet 'people's capitalism' has been a narrow affair. Share ownership is still confined to a minority and' while many of these have benefited from windfall profits from the sale of undervalued public assets, a genuine citizen's stake in Great Britain plc is still a long way off. Indeed, the evidence is that many who bought small stakes in the privatisation bonanza quickly sold them off for short-term gain and the shareholding of privatised utilities is now being concentrated back in the hands of the big institutions, many of them based overseas. Meanwhile, though some citizens have benefited handsomely, it is the City and the financial institutions who have benefited most.

We could be much more radical about popular share ownership – we could give every citizen a stake in our economy. I would like to see a Citizens' Unit Trust or Universal Share Option Programme (USOP) established in which every adult citizen has a stake.

Much thinking has already been done on this. In 1984 Stuart Speiser proposed a USOP in which every US citizen would, over twenty years, aquire (through a government guaranteed loan scheme, repaid through earnings on the assets) a $100,000 share in US industry. This stake would be obtained from new productive assets purchased by industry. Speiser arrived at the $100,000 figure by dividing the 50 million US families into the $5 trillion that US business will spend on new productive assets in the next twenty years. He calculated that each $100,000 share in what he called a 'Superstock' plan would yield $20,000 in guaranteed annual income.

In effect, the Speiser plan uses the conventional system for buying new stock, but applies it to every citizen. At present, if share speculators wish to buy new stock and do not have the cash to do it, they go to the bank for a loan, offer existing stock as collateral and then pay off the loan through earnings on the assets they are acquiring. Applying exactly this principle, under the Superstock plan, the government guarantees the loan that each family secures as it acquires an increasing share of equity in new capital investment. The system is by no means new. Exactly the same principle was applied in the Second World War to help US veterans obtain housing through mortgages guaranteed by government. Speiser proposes his scheme as a comprehensive and radical alternative to the current basis of our welfare system which depends on 'transfer payments' being made, effectively, from the rich to the poor. In essence, what he suggests is that, instead of government sponsored redistribution of wealth, there should be a government organised redistribution of assets. This seems to me to be placing too much weight on what is, nevertheless, an interesting concept.

In the UK, Nobel Prize winner Professor James Meade has been working on a more limited, but more practical version of the same idea. His suggestion, which builds on a model already operating in Sweden, is for a 'Citizens' Share Ownership Unit Trust' which owns 10 per cent of all private sector enterprises over a given size. Shares in the Trust are created in two ways. First by requiring companies to issue new shares to the Trust every year, either through scrip issue or by using a proportion of the profits. And secondly by handing over a substantial share of state owned industries (chiefly the utilities) either direct from the public sector, or in the process of privatisation. Professor Mead calculates that, over twenty years the Trust would build up a stake amounting to around 10 per cent of the enterprises involved and around 60 per cent of the shares in the utility industries. Dividends to each citizen would amount to between £100 and £150 per year – which is a small, but important start down the road to a 'Citizens Unit Trust'.

Both of these schemes have important beneficial side effects. They could, in the end, reduce the need for welfare based transfer payments, as shares begin to generate income. They offer the possibility of both national and community variants, with the latter opening up access to capital markets for community based enterprises and small businesses which are not, at present, readily accessible to them. They could provide a mechanism for all to share in the fruits of the new technology in an era where there is a real danger of concentration of productive and wealth producing power in fewer and fewer hands. But the real benefit of a 'Citizens' Unit Trust' lies in the fact that it provides a mechanism of create a real, rather than make-believe citizens' capitalism, creating powerful instrument for re-distribution and giving us an industrial base which would be more in the ownership of the citizen, and less in the hands of the huge institutions and the state.

A MARKET FOR THE CONSUMER

The history of the twentieth century shows that democracy cannot thrive without a free market economy. It also shows that many countries which espouse free enterprise are not democracies. For example, South Africa and several South American dictatorships have been staunch upholders of free enterprise and political repression. Indeed, it is not without significance that, when asked to list the freedoms she claims to have brought to Britain, Mrs Thatcher herself always defines them in economic terms, never in political ones.

However, while economic freedom is only a part of the full package of citizenship, it is, nevertheless, an important part. We should remember that in the new industrial age there will be a major concentration of productive capacity, with more production power in fewer hands. So consumer interests are increasingly important. The producer powers (industrial confederations and trade unions) which have shaped our society in the past should be balanced by consumer power in the future.

Power can easily be concentrated at the top of a society when governments collude with monopoly interests, large corporations and privileged groups. In Citadel Britain, state power and high finance conspire to dominate a mass of weak and isolated individual consumers and citizens. In Citizens' Britain, consumers, like voters, have information and influence on decisions.

Just as constitutional reform is necessary to ensure the citizen's status within the political system, so consumer reform is needed to give power to the citizen in the market place. Concern about the quality of food and about the health risks of certain products has led consumers to organise and assert their interests. It is intereting to note, for example, that there are over three times as many members of the Consumers' Association as there are in the Labour Party. And consumers of health and welfare services (carers, patients, disabled people) are already organising and demanding a say in the planning and running of these services. These movements should be strengthened and encouraged.

Incidentally, placing placing power in the hands of the consumer is entirely consistent with the enviromental need to create a more sustainable economy. Given a choice, the consumer will always choose quality and product life, rather than the planned obsolescence which is of benefit to the manufacturer and marketer. Indeed, consumer power is probably the most effective force which will ensure that we abandon the 'chuck it away' society in favour of sustainability and quality.

There are two things which need to be done to give consumers more power. The first is to be ruthless in attacking monopolies. The second is to be courageous in enhancing the power of the individual consumer.

Current practice on monopolies makes judgements on would-be takeovers on the negative basis that anything is permitted which can be proved not to damage competition. We should reverse this to a positive criterion, requiring any takeover which will result in more than, say, 20 per cent of the market to prove that the result will positively enhance competition. Establishing such a criterion will be more difficult after 1992 because of the size of the European market and the fact that making accurate measurements of market share in other European nations is not as easy as it is in Britain. But Europe must get its act together on this. Ensuring competition will be even more vital in the larger European market than it is in Britain today. In strengthening the power of the consumer, five basic principles should apply:

Access Without equal access to the market all other consumer rights fall.

Choice Without choice there will be no economic stimulus to make the producers more efficient and responsive and no chance to establish a fair market price.

Information Without information the consumer cannot make informedchoices. It is here that our present government fails so significantly. Even now, despite the tragedies of Bradford, Kings Cross and Zeebrugge, we are still denied access to information from fire authorities and health officers relating to safety in public places. We know, for instance, that some cross channel ferries have still not come up to post Zeebrugge standards of safety, but we are not allowed to know which ones.

Redress Swift, efficient and adequate, backed by ready access to the legal system when it is required.

Safety To enable consumers to be confident that what they purchase will not subject them to risks which they are unaware of.

Here are some proposals which we could immediately implement:

* Establish a single powerful national utilities watchdog body to

oversee all utilities and public services, combining the functions of OFGAS, OFTEC and other bodies established to oversee the utility industries. Combine the Monopolies & Mergers Commission and the Office of Fair Trading into a single body, independent from the DTI, whose remit is to promote, protect and enhance competition and attack monopoly in either the public or private sector. Wherever a monopoly can be broken up, it should be. New entrants should be actively encouraged and supported (see 'Making small businesses big and big businesses small'). Where a 'natural' monopoly (for example, in the utility industries) is kept in the public sector, franchising and contracting out of services should be required, wherever possible.

* Establish specific rights of access to consumer information.

* Strengthen consumer rights of redress and back them up with legal sanctions. Permit 'class action' legal cases in consumer matters.

* Strengthen the scope, states and financial resources of the National Consumer Council (NCC). The NCC should be equipped to conduct scientific product tests, should be empowered to require companies to release details of specified products and processes and should be able to publish these. It should also be able to support or take up legal cases on behalf of individuals on consumer matters where these have 'test case' status.

* Promote and enforce standards of quality, with statutory established periods of guarantee (3 years for a car? 5 years for a fridge?)

* Enforce labelling requirements, both in respect to contents and to make possible direct easy comparisons to be made between competing goods as to price and weight (this would follow much continental practice which requires food to be labelled showing the price per 100g.)

* Place much more stringent requirements on packaging, requiring returnability where practical and environmental safeguards where this is not possible.

NATIONALISE OR PRIVATISE?

A Question of Ownership or a Question of Service?

Ever since the war, controversy has raged between the Conservative and Labour parties about the transfer of major industries from the public to the private sector and vice versa. Conservative and Labour governments have taken office pledged to denationalise or nationalise, regardless of the devastating damage done to some of our most important industries by constant change or threat of change. To me, much of this argument has seemed profoundly irresponsible and irrelevant when compared with the far more important issues affecting the conduct of the industries and their service to their consumers.

Apart from the 1945 Labour administration, no government has thrust this issue so prominently to the forefront of its policies as the Thatcher administrations. They have made no bones about the their ideological commitment to eliminate public sector industry once and for all, and increasingly they have come to rely on the proceeds of sales of these industries to prop up their financial policies and to make room for pre-election tax cuts. The blind ideological commitment and the short-sighted financial expediency of this approach is as bad for Britain as was the contrasting Labour obsession with nationalisation and the excessive power Labour conferred on trade unions.

Labour's review has moved the party onto Mrs Thatcher's ground, with a few changes to soften the edges and a brief nostalgic glance backward at British Telecom and water, which they intend to renationalise.

Both parties have totally missed the point.

Clearly, there are some institutions which are or would be better off in the private sector (British Airways is one, Rolls Royce is another), just as our utility industries, or at least the major part of them (see below), are probably more approriately placed in the public sector. But I have always thought that the question 'Who owns?' is far less important than the question 'How is the public served?'. For me, therefore, the foremost considerations are the satisfaction of the consumer, the interests of the economy and the motivation of those working in the industry.

The consumer wants good choice, security of supply, good quality and service, reasonable price and an effective remedy for complaints.

The interests of the economy require efficiently run industries, using resources efficiently and providing first rate support for other parts of the economy dependent on their services.

The employee would have involvement in the enterprise and terms of employment which encourage commitment and efficiency.

The best way to satisfy these key requirements is to emphasise:

Maximum competition where this is possible and consistent with the nature of the business.

Maximum decentralisation of large corporations to bring them closer to the consumer, to facilitate employee involvement and to encourage local decision making.

I do not dissent from the general proposition that transfer of ownership from the public to the private sector may lead to greater efficiency, greater freedom from government interference and greater opportunity for employee involvement and commitment. Much depends upon the extent of the competition possible and the extent of government's unavoidable regulation of the industry, for example for health and environmental reasons. In making a decision to change ownership it is also necessary to calculate the cost and upheaval of transferring ownership from the public to the private sector or vice versa.

So here are the criteria against which to decide whether particular proposals for nationalisation or privatisation are appropriate.

Does the consumer stand to benefit, on a continuing basis, in terms of service, quality, choice and cost?

Is there a cogent reason for expecting efficiency to be improved?

Will the industry's employees have the opportunity of obtaining and retaining a substantial share holding in the business?

Where monopoly conditions are likely, is a regulatory body going to be created which is easy and cheap to approach and quick and effective in action?

Is it a strategic industry?

Should it be retained in British hands?

Are effective competition and efficient services likely to be the result?

And here are some thoughts which should guide what ought to happen to those industries which this government has already privatised.

Change of ownership of basic industries, either nationalisation or privatisation, is disruptive. It may also be wasteful and irrelevant. It should never be embarked upon for ideological reasons.

The cost of taking back into public ownership industries already privatised would be immense and, with other pressing demands for expenditure, it should be avoided unless monopoly power is clearly being abused and this cannot be prevented, except by a return to the public sector.

Competition must be stimulated to the maximum extent, particularly in industries where the scope for technical innovation is great or where the industry's management or the unions could exercise excessive power. Regulatory bodies should be given the power to protect the interests of weaker competitors and of consumers and to uphold safety and quality standards. Decentralisation should be required in large monopolisitic industries in the public service field, whether in public or private ownership.

Action should be taken to increase employee ownership in industries already returned to the private sector. The aim should be to have 10 per cent of shares in employee hands. Share offers to employees would take priority in further share disposals or issues, and taxation arrangements would be reviewed to facilitate this policy.

Consumers should also be given a stake in all privatised monopoly utilities. We should hand over a minority (perhaps 30 per cent) of shares to customers of utilities which are privatised. These shares would not be saleable, but would attract dividends and carry with them voting rights. These 'customer shares' should be used to elect customer representatives onto the relevent boards of management. In this way privatised public utilities will continue genuinely to belong to the public they serve, rather than to share speculators whose primary interest is, naturally, in profit, not service.

A comprehensive regulatory body for all public utilities, whether in public or private hands, should be established, to protect the consumer and preserve the public interest.

Meanwhile, we must look again at our attitude to utilities and industry left in the public sector. The public corporation as administered in Britain has not satisfied either government, management, the public or the employees. Pricing and the financial regime of the day have been used repeatedly for purposes which have little to do with business and efficiency; limitations on freedom to raise capital have interfered with the proper extension, renewal and maintenance of the assets of the industries; and neither the public nor Parliament have been satisfied with the accountability of the industries concerned, or of ministers who are supposed to be responsible for them. These fundamental issues should be examined again with the following in mind:

* reformulation of responsibilities of the boards and of Ministers in respect of policy, finance and management in order to eliminate

arbitrary political interference, establish clearcut accountability and create conditions for efficiency;

* investigating different forms of public ownership such as the Company Acts model, to deter interference in management and facilitate employee shareholding and participation;

* establishing a contractual basis for the appointment of board members. One other thought.

There is often a real case for privatising some element of a public utility, even where there is none for privatising all of it. A principle which can apply here is that of the 'common carrier'. An example of the 'common carrier' system is our road network. The public owns the roads, but anyone can drive on them provided they are qualified, their car is safe and they obey the rules. We could have applied the same principle to British Telecom, keeping the network in public hands but allowing maximum private competition in what happens at either end (the phone, faxes, teleprinters and so on) and in value-added services using the system. We could have applied it, in the same way, to electricity, allowing private power generation to use the public grid – or to gas, or (just about) to water. We could even consider its application, still, to rail – with the rail network left in public ownership and private carrying companies, large and small, free to use it, subject to the necessary regulation to ensure safety and customer service.

The post-war industrial/political scene has been wracked by the obsession of Conservative and Labour politicians with conflicting views on the ownership of some of our most important industries. I do not accept the crude and stark claims Tories and Socialists make for one form of industrial organisation against the other. For the great mass of customers and of employees, ownership is of little or no account. What matters for them is quality of service, price, accessibility and job satisfaction. I think they are right.

MAKING SMALL BUSINESSES BIG AND BIG BUSINESSES SMALL

One of the things I am proudest to have done since I was elected an MP is to have worked with others in Yeovil to start an Enterprise

Agency, helping small businesses. When in 1986, at the height of the Westland crisis, that great Yeovil firm had to make more than 1,000 people redundant, I watched in fear at what would happen to our unemployment. It hardly went up at all. Almost every worker who lost his or her job was quickly able to find another – hundreds of them went to the Enterprise Agency, who helped them set up by themselves.

One of the respects in which I pay tribute to Mrs Thatcher is the way she has encouraged enterprise in Britain. My criticism of her is that she has not gone fast enough, or far enough. Britain still has one of the smallest small business sectors among the advanced economies. The importance of small businesses and self-employment to me are not just economic. Someone who is self-employed or owns his or her own job has their own economic freedom in their own hands – and that's what I want to see. So I think we can go much further than Mrs Thatcher in encouraging self employment and small business.

Probably no single reform will encourage self-employment and personal enterprise more than the introduction of a Basic Income, since this will give the citizen a form of social independence which enables economic independence, as well.

There are other things we could do, too. Here are some of them:

1 Define exactly what a small business is and then

2 Require a percentage of all local and national government purchasing to be placed with small businesses, preferably local ones (they do this in the US).

3 Treat incorporated and unincorporated businesses on the same basis.

4 Introduce a code of practise for prompt payment of bills and be prepared to give it statutory authority if large firms don't observe it.

5 Do the same for the very unfair practise of discriminatory discounting which is doing such damage to small retail outlets. Under this practise, large grocery chains use their buying power to demand from suppliers uneconomic discounts which are then paid for by charging higher prices to small retail shops (it's illegal in the US).

6 Require the banks to decentralise their operations so that more investment decisions are made locally. And set them targets for small business lending.

7 Change the ridiculous conditions for the Enterprise Allowance, so that it is easier to get.

8 Require banks to take a 'fixed and floating' charge in businesses

and forbid them to ask small businessmen to put their car and house on the line for a loan (it's illegal in the US).

9 Provide tax incentives for small business owners who want to hand over their firm to their employees, rather than keeping it in the family.

10 Provide more support and advice to small business at the crucial point where they are considering expansion.

We are very good at helping start up, where nine tenths of the assistance goes. But it is at the point of expansion that the real leap in turnover and employment occurs. And it is here where far too many good businesses founder.

Helping small businesses grow big is only one side of it. We ought also to be helping big businesses break up into smaller ones, too. There is tendency for big companies to get bigger, both by internal growth and acquisition. Sometimes it is necessary to compete on the European or world stage. In other cases it leads to concentration of power and inefficiencies.

Of course, we should support the profitable expansion of companies where this is in the best long-term interests of the country. However, in order to ensure the continued survival and expansion of smaller and medium sized companies, we should also encourage small businesses within big companies to break out and become independent.

Some companies can become too big. Where that involves the creation of monopoly power we look to the Monopolies and Mergers Board and the European Commission to protect the interests of society as a whole. But other companies can be too big without being what the law regards as a monopoly. They can cover a lot of different activities, or they can cover activities that you or I would say are similar, but the law does not. For example, companies can control a lot of newspapers, magazines, TV stations, cable TV, satellite broadcasting, and so on. They may not infringe the monopolies legislation, but it can, rightly, give cause for concern.

There are two traditional ways of controlling excessive size. One approach is to force a company to sell off some activities. But the company making the sale does not actually become any less powerful; it merely reduces its assets and increases its cash. That may not be in the best interests of the shareholders or the country, especially if the company does not use the money for reinvestment, but puts it aside in a cash mountain in order to be even more predatory in the merger market-place.

The other approach is to take part of a company without full compensation. The original company certainly is now smaller, but it has been robbed.

There is another way, a way to control size automatically, using the free market itself to ensure efficiency, whilst making sure that the outcome is just to all parties. I will call it 'demerger' and this is how it works. Any company is owned by its shareholders. A large company is normally a collection of companies, or seperate businesses organised in divisions. All are owned by the ultimate shareholders.

Demerger allows one company in a group to leave that group. When it becomes a separate company, all the shareholders in the original group are given shares in the new company pro rata to their shareholding in the original group. Here is an example.

MultiGroup plc has 10 companies, one of them called QuickCo Ltd. QuickCo demerges from MultiGroup. Each shareholder will now have one share in QuickCo for every one share in MultiGroup. QuickCo is now an independent company. It is unrelated to Multi-Group. However, the same shareholders own both companies. They can sell their shares as and when they want. Each company can call on its shareholders for fresh capital as and when it wants. The original MultiGroup is now smaller; it has 'lost' QuickCo. But nothing has been taken without compensation, as the real owners, the share-holders, got shares in QuickCo. We now have a new, small company in the market: QuickCo.

Who benefits? Pretty well everyone, is the answer.

Shareholders have retained ownership of both companies (at least until they choose to sell their shares). They have a greater variety of investment. If QuickCo can become a major success by being independent and unconstrained, then shareholders should do better.

The management of QuickCo is now independent, as a smaller, more agile company.

MultiGroup can concentrate on its remaining activities without distraction.

The financial institutions should be happy, as there is now an extra public company in being, with more shares to be marketed. These institutions need to see a constant flow of new companies coming on the market if their business is to grow.

The country certainly benefits. We have a new independent company and more employment, enterprise and wealth creation as a result.

So here is what we should do. First, publicise the facility. Second, give the management of every subsidiary company or business the right to appeal to the ultimate shareholders of their parent company if they are being prevented from demerging by the parent company board. Third, ensure that the management has the ability to prepare a case for demerger and for this to be sent to shareholders and be discussed at a shareholders meeting. Of course, the board of the top company would have the equal right to put their case against it, if they were not in favour. We would have to set up some safeguards, such as the protection of management making such an application against dismissal, while this is in process.

The shareholders themselves will take the final decision. All we have done is to ensure that market forces have an opportunity to work. It is interesting to note, incidentally, that many of the most successful new-technology companies are recognising the benefits of demerger in increasing efficiency and motivation. Some time ago Rank Xerox began to encourage its best software programmers to go self employed, with assistance from the company and a promise of future business. The result was in increase in productivity and a decrease in personnel problems.

16

The Law

Those who like sausages and respect the law should take care to watch neither of them being made.

Anon

Access to Justice

It is the first right of the citizen to have access to justice, and the first duty of government to provide it. Since the Second World War, however, the law in Britain has become much more complex and in many ways more distant from the citizen. Our legal system is now a minefield of rights and wrongs, crimes and torts, opportunities and regulations. The result has been an exponential rise in the number of lawyers. The barrister or solicitor in, say, 1946 was able to give expert advice on large swathes of the law; today the lawyer is weighed under by burgeoning legislation. He has either to be a specialist in a limited range or obtain specialist advice from experts.

At the end of the last war there were no industrial tribunals, social security appeal tribunals or value added tax tribunals. Labour law was simple. Judicial review was thought to be available only rarely. Matrimonial financial law was still founded upon simple principles. White-collar crime was rare, and usually based upon easily detectable frauds – for the personal computer had yet to be invented.

Here are some things which should be considered to improve the operation of the law in Citizens' Britain.

Legal Aid

In theory, legal aid ranks alongside the National Health Service as a major social innovation. But in practise, like the NHS, state education and welfare, it is weighed down by bureaucracy, under funding and the growing complexity of modern life.

The limited introduction of legal aid in 1948, and its extension in 1964, was designed to give the ordinary member of the public access to justice which previously had not been available because of cost. The trade unions had for years organised effective legal assistance schemes for those injured at work. However, it was virtually impossible for the citizen of modest means to sue for the declaration of rights or the payment of compensataion, or to have a reasonable choice of a lawyer to defend him on a criminal charge.

It is fair to accept that successive governments have increased expenditure on legal aid. Regrettably, however, it is far from enough to point simply to financial statistics. We must start by examining our beliefs, for nothing stems more directly from political principle and philosophy than our attitude to justice. I am utterly clear about mine.

Laws may change but justice must be immutable. It must be indivisible, too. We cannot allow justice to be divided on a class basis or to be better for the rich than it is for the poor. All citizens, whatever their position, must be able to use the law to enjoy their rights and to defend themselves against wrong. Does our law in Britain meet these standards today? The plain answer is no.

Take one example, industrial tribunals. The Labour Party when in government establised the industrial tribunals system. It chose deliberately to refuse legal aid for them. The reason, as so often, lies in the influence of the trade unions – for trade-union officials were fearful for their membership figures if the tribunals removed a good reason for remaining a union member. For other reasons, principally to protect the unscrupulous employer from scrutiny by an independent tribunal, the Tory government from 1979 followed the Labour Party inthis cosy conspiracy to deny the ordinary citizen access to justice in the workplace. What are the consequences? Day by day, employees either fail to bring their cases to industrial tribunals, because they are afraid to attend themselves, or they appear and are often represented inadequately. This is an example of how justice can be indivisible in principle but divided in practise.

The industrial tribunals are not the only example of the legal aid gap. The same point applies with equal force, as I see almost every week in my constituency surgery, to social security appeal tribunals, whose determinations often make the difference between a basic living standard and abject poverty.

I am convinced that the failure to extend legal aid to these tribunals must be remedied. It is fundamentally illiberal. It demands of the nervous and inexperienced litigant a giant killing act besides which even the historic achievements of my home football team Yeovil Town pale into insignificance!

Defamation of character is another very obvious area in which there is no access to the law for people other than the very wealthy. Parents falsely accused by a newspaper of abusing their children, a doctor maliciously accused of indecency by a patient, a councillor pilloried without justification in the council chamber for improper motives – too frequently many of these cannot contemplate an action for defamation, because of the cost.

The reason for this is twofold. First, no legal aid is available for defamation proceedings. Second, specialist libel solicitors sometimes charge huge hourly rates for their advice; and barristers' fees in defamation cases, though often better value in terms of unit cost, add substantially to the bills. The protection of a person's reputation may well be essential for personal and business reasons. The active citizen should not be maimed by financial discrimination. If these high legal costs can be justified at all, then, by simple logic, there is justification for their payment by the Legal Aid Board.

If we are to base our system for providing access to justice on legal aid, then it must be both comprehensive and properly funded.

A Statute of Rights

There are some even more fundamental failures of the legal system. Why have successive governments been so afraid of the European Convention on Human Rights? Why is the United Kingdom determined to be the black sheep of Europe, bucking the trend and refusing to incorporate the Convention into our domestic law? Why have successive governments placed on the aggrieved citizen the burden of having to go, unaided financially, to a court in distant Strasbourg to enforce fundamental freedoms. For example, the right to undisturbed family life, the right not to have one's telephone tapped save in extreme circumstances, the right not to have one's property appropriated by the government, the right, as a woman, to be treated equally with men in the welfare system. All of these have been rights which the Strasburg court has upheld for British citizens because our own courts would not.

In a nation of active citizens, the judges should be at least as active in promoting rights under the Convention as the citizen in claiming them. Whether in Berwick, Burnley or Bristol, the citizen would be able to rely upon the Convention rights in every court and tribunal in the land and in every cause or matter. It would be possible to go to the local county court, with legal aid, for a declaration of those rights where necessary. The embodiment of fundamental freedoms in a Statute of Rights is a prerequisite of sensible and necessary constitutional progress and reform. It is not enough merely to enact the statute; it must be as easily enforceable as I have described.

Some of our foremost constitutional commentators have given their weight to the reasoning behind the campaign for a Statute of Rights, accessible and enforceable. Foremost amongst them have been Roy Jenkins, Anthony Lester and Lord Hailsham. The last, a distinguished and experienced Conservative parliamentarian, lawyer and (twice) Lord Chancellor, is perhaps best qualified as our guide. His experience in the House of Commons has led him to the conclusion that the House and its individual members are simply no longer able to protect the individual citizen from infringement of rights and liberties. Parliament has become too complex, too overworked and buried in legislation and too political. Lord Hailsham has warned urgently, in the context of a Labour government, of the dangers of 'elective dictatorship'. I agree with him and note that his arguments are even more applicable after ten years of government by his own party.

The Right to Privacy

The active citizen should be entitled to carry on his private activities in private. United Kingdom laws do not protect that privacy. Subject to overriding public interest considerations, which must be retained, the enabling state which I envisage will introduce new laws to protect privacy from the prurience of the press. I do not, at present, favour a statutory right of reply, but I do believe that we must ensure that the

Press Council becomes fully effective and has the power to redress invasion of privacy.

Reform of the Legal Profession

Of course all the principles, rights and freedoms are worth little if those who need to enforce them cannot gain access to the professionals who will win enforcement for them. What we must ensure is that the legal profession is cost effective, available, independent and highly professional.

There is no magic formula for solving the continuing and unseemly disagreements between the branches of the legal profession. What they must understand is that the consumer, not the lawyer, comes first. Lawyers have the capacity to respond to this priority and still make an adequate living. Their response should be to cut away the undergrowth of rules and archaisms which have stifled the modernisation of the profession. This can be achieved without undermining professional independence.

Law Centres

Law centres have played a key role in the modernisation of the law and its accessibility. Solicitors in conventional private practice are rarely attracted to neighbourhoods where the work is dependent upon legal aid, and includes much for which no payment is available. As a result, law centres have come to the fore in inner city areas. They tend to be staffed by very bright young lawyers, often barristers as well as solicitors. They have been constituted on a basis which means that every client is advised, whatever the nature of the work. They have funded many important cases in the fields of housing, civil liberties and judicial review. They have been able to draw upon ready specialist support from the Bar and sympathetic solicitors, as well as from national organisations such as Liberty (NCCL) and the Legal ActionGroup.

After some initial tolerance, the Thatcher government took against law centres. They became perceived by Tory Ministers as politically motivated and left-wing. This simplistic judgement may or may not be accurate in terms of the political views of law centre workers. If it is, it reflects the sad fact that few young right-wingers have been prepared to work in the centres, and perhaps prefer the extraordinary salaries available to young solicitors in the larger London firms. There is, however, no credible evidence of political bias in the conduct of the centres.

As a result of changing government policy, law centres were deprived of funds by national government and by local authorities under central government pressure. Many became non-viable. This happened as the need for law centres increased; indeed, there is now a case for a network of law centres to serve rural areas too, where the existing lawyers often display a lack of legal knowledge of welfare and housing legislation and are unable to perform tribunal work free of charge.

Such needs must be met. The provision of a network of law centres where necessary should be the joint responsibility of central and local government. We need to co-ordinate access to and administration of the law with the facilities and services of voluntary organisations such as Citizens' Advice Bureaux and the statutory functions carried on by local authorities, notably the administration and enforcement of trading standards.

A Ministry of Justice

Of course, it is of little use providing a network of law centres, wider legal aid and more competitive lawyers if the citizen fears a conspiracy between law enforcers and government. The separation of powers, upon which our fragile constitutional conventions are based, has seemed under threat during the 1980s. This perception, even if unjustified, undermines public confidence in the rule of law itself. The position of the Attorney General has become a nonsense. However able, however capable of directing himself scrupulously in his differing roles, it has become clear that it is unacceptable for one person, and an MP and minister at that, to act simultaneously as the government's chief legal adviser (which includes a political role) and as impartial head of the prosecution service. The position during the Westland affair of the then Attorney-General' Sir Michael Havers QC, and especially of his Solicitor-General, Sir Patrick Mayhew QC, bears evidence of this.

We should now learn from the experience of our partners in Europe and create a Ministry of Justice, with an accountable political head – a Cabinet Minister in the House of Commons. His department would take existing functions from the monolith of the Home Office and from the Lord Chancellor's Department.

The Attorney General's independent tasks would be carried on outside the political arena. The Lord Chancellor would be a non-political head of the whole judiciary, appointing judges by way of an independent commission. The arcane mysteries of present-day judicial appointment are no longer an acceptable or accountable route to judicial office.

The Judiciary

The Judicial Studies Board has done much to improve the training of judges. More needs to be done. The establishment of a judicial staff college, based perhaps at the Civil Service College, would provide for consistent and compulsory continuing education for full-time and-part-time judges.

The judiciary should be more in touch with the world of the young. This is not to say that the bench should be occupied by middle-aged 'swingers'. However, there is a great deal to be said for judges with their own current or recent experience of teenagers. We should be aiming at recruiting good lawyers as part-time judges by the age of 40, and making full-time appointments at around 45 years. Women judges and those from the ethnic minorities do exist, but still in disproportionately low numbers. All judges trying cases at first instance (below appeal level) should retire not later than their 65th birthday.

I believe that these requirements for the reform of the judiciary are self-evident, yet successive Labour and Conservative governments have failed to act upon them. I have become accustomed to hearing Labour MPs, in particular, complaining that judges are out of touch. Then why did their government do so little to provide the remedy in the years 1964-70, and 1974-9?

In this chapter I have not sought to set out a blueprint for legal reform. That would be the task of the Ministry of Justice, but we must ensure that the veil of vested interests, traditions, and restrictions in the operation of the law in Britain is pulled aside. The law should be accessible, determined and, above all, just. For justice is the fountainhead of a civilised, pluralist society.

17

Foreign Policy

The age of nations is past. The task before us now if we would not perish is to build the earth.

Pierre Teilhard De Chardin

I decided to go into politics in 1976 when I was a diplomat in the United Kingdom Mission to the United Nations in Geneva. One of the chief reasons for my decision was a growing conviction that Britain was following the wrong course internationally. Traditional British isolationism persisted in infecting our foreign policy. In a world where the need for an internationalist approach and the recognition of global interdependence would grow, we were in danger of being left out and left behind.

The worst fears I had then have been all too damagingly realised. Thanks to the isolationism of the present government, Britain is now being left on the sidelines. It must be a matter of profound concern to all those who believe that Britain has an important part to play in the creation of a more stable and peaceful Europe and in the reshaping of the East/West relationship that both the US and the USSR now see West Germany as the heart of this process and Britain as almost irrelevant to it.

New opportunities for dialogue and negotiation in Europe are opening up. The prospect of a strong and prosperous European continent, including the hitherto submerged countries of the Soviet bloc, is beckoning. West Germany has everything to gain – economically as well as in terms of eventual possible reunification – from direct talks with the USSR and her neighbours. Britain can either try to halt this process, and risk missing a historic opportunity, or we can advance it and strengthen our own European ties.

This is but one tiny example of the phenomenon that I have been commenting on throughout this book – that we are living in an era of profound change.

The old pattern of world power is changing, too, and so are the issues at the centre of world politics. Compared with a generation ago, the world has become much smaller, much more delicately balanced and much more crowded. It is clear that we will need an entirely new map of the world to guide British foreign policy through the 1990s. The old comfortable certainties of the post-war era just won't do.

There is nothing more absurd than the Prime Minister's nostalgia for the golden years of the Anglo-American partnership at the end of the Second World War. Except perhaps her absurd defence of the nineteenth century myths of British sovereignty. Faced with the challenges of the 1990s, Mrs Thatcher stands looking determinedly behind her. She seems scared of change – scared of developments in Europe, scared of a loosening relationship with Washington, fearful of the international co-operation which will be the only way to operate effectively in a highly interdependent world.

What we need is a forward-looking vision of Britain's role in the world. A role which enables this country to move with change instead of always striving vainly to block it.

Three powerful currents are pushing along the quickening tide of change: the growing confidence within Western Europe in our developing European identity, the shift in relations between the superpowers, and the growing economic power of the developing world, especially the Pacific Basin. Here are some ways in which these changes will affect us.

Europe

A stronger, more united Western Europe with a clearer idea of its own international interests will unavoidably find that its priorities differ from those of the United States.

I recognise the dangers of being too optimistic about the continuation of Mr Gorbachov's policies. We have to be cautious and we have to move step by step, but the whole process of glasnost and perestroika in the USSR responds to underlying changes in the Soviet economy and society. It will not be possible simply to put the clock back as some of the Conservative Party's cold warriors would have us believe.

They seem to forget that twenty years ago, in the Harmel Report, Great Britain and its allies reaffirmed the dual aims of the alliance: to maintain sufficient forces to deter the threat while at the same time working through diplomacy to build a different pattern of relations between East and West.

We must now be true to those aims, not remain frozen in the attitudes of the cold war.

The new climate gives new opportunities to cut arms. It also makes more urgent the establishment of a twin-pillar NATO, with Europe bearing more of the burden of its own defence. Of course, we recognise that the United States will continue to be vital to the effectiveness of NATO and to the defence of Europe, but the really important long-term dialogue for us is with our neighbours in Eastern Europe. This is the new dimension to our European vision; the vision of a wider Europe, a Europe form Dublin to Lublin, a Europe without the superpowers. We need a much more open and progressive dialogue with the nations of what we now call Eastern Europe, nations such as Hungary, and to a lesser extent Poland, which are making such remarkable progress towards liberalising their societies.

It will not be easy for Europe to develop a sensible economic response to changes in Eastern Europe. The thrust of economic as well as political change can only come from within each East European country. What we must do is to encourage such changes, to develop the widest political, cultural and especially economic links. We should welcome moves from countries such as Austria and Hungary to create a wider Europe, starting with accepting them as associate members of the EEC. Above all, we have to respond as a coherent Western European group, not collapse into squabbles over future markets or particular political interests. To meet this danger the European Community should now urgently establish a European Development Agency for co-ordinating our economic response to the East.

Our defence policies too must be firmly set, not by the old attitudes of the cold war but within these new political realities. In the uncertain conditions of Gorbachov's glasnost and the continuing strength of the Warsaw Pact, there are some hard choices to be made on the nuclear component of Western defence. And if the two superpowers eventually do commit themselves to deep cuts in their own deterrent forces, there are some hard choices to be made about the point at which Britain's own nuclear forces should be included in disarmament negotiations. This includes, of course, Trident.

Trident was never desirable, but by the time of the next election that will be yesterday's argument. With the Trident system well on its way to deployment, we will face different questions. The chief of them is this: what role will the British deterrent play in the security of Western Europe, and what influence could it play in the progressive reduction of arms levels?

The policy on which the old Alliance parties fought the last election still seems to me the only rational approach. Britain must maintain the forces necessary to meet potential threats, but we must also work with our neighbours in the pursuit of both defence and disarmament.

Trident is not the only question we must face. We must also address ourselves to the whole issue of the modernisation of our tactical and intermediate weapons. I do not believe that it is either sensible or right to maintain any weapons system which is out of date. I accept that this is, or soon will be, the case for some weapons. We must not therefore shirk the need for modernisation, when necessary.

Military decisions must be taken within a prevailing political climate, and the climate at present is one of progress and hope. As the West German Foreign Minister, Hans Deitrich Genscher, has so frequently pointed out, to commit the alliance irrevocably to modernise at the moment, when progress towards disarmament is going so well, would be unnecessary, unwise and destructive. Modernisation is even more irrelevant and disruptive if, following the Gorbachov and Bush initiatives, NATO and Warsaw Pact conventional forces are to move to parity by 1992. After all, as Mrs Thatcher has repeatedly told us, the only reason for having short range nuclear forces is to counter Soviet conventional superiority. So if the latter disappears, so, logically, must the former.

Further ahead still there is the question of nuclear weapons within the European pillar. Again, it is vital to deal with the realities. And the reality is that nuclear weapons will have to play a role in European security for some time yet. But we must not allow the possibilities of a Europe which is free of nuclear weapons to be banished from our horizon. It was Aristotle who said: 'Our hopes are rarely realised, but it is our pursuit of them which changes the course of history'. We must never lose hope that we can change the course of history in Europe; that the twentieth century, which Europe has soaked in blood, will give way to a twenty first century in which the great power, imagination and skill of the European people can be turned to the creation of a peace which does not rest for its survival upon nuclear terror.

A Multi-sided Pattern of Power

The world outside Europe is also changing fast. One of the great engines of that change is the growing economic power of the nations of the Pacific rim. What is rather less realised is that economic power is always followed by political influence and, regrettably, military power as well. I see no reason why this immutable law should be changed in the case of the nations of the Pacific Basin.

The United States already looks to the Pacific as an area of influence and importance, at least as much as it does to the Atlantic. Indeed, for the businessman in California, what happens in Tokyo is much more important than what happens in Brussels, Paris, or London.

If we are to look in the future to a much more multi-sided world, then we must recognise that the centres of power no longer lie just on the edges of the Atlantic ocean but around the Pacific as well. It will take considerable wisdom to adjust to this shift. The relationship between the United States and Europe will continue to be vital for our political and economic interests. But there are destructive forces on both sides of the Atlantic which could easily endanger it.

I am glad that we now have a president in the White House who appears to be both more sensitive and more delicate than his predecessor in his handling of international affairs, though I am bound to add that this is not very difficult.

Equally, on our side of the Atlantic, we must not let the forces of anti-Americanism take charge. If we approach the whole question of the Atlantic relationship in a new spirit we must approach our broader relations with other areas of the world in a new spirit also. It must be right for us to work for a much more multi-sided and stable pattern of world power. This means that our task in the future will be to help and encourage the growth of cohesion amongst other groups in the world. If I were to pick out a single area where there is a real benefit of encouraging regional cohesion it is South America. The nations of South America have been trying to ensure that they remain non-aligned. It is entirely in our interests that they should succeed.

The Problem of Debt

The recent strengthening of democracy in South America has been one of the most hopeful international signs in recent years, but there are worrying indications that all this is coming to an end. The burden of high debt has handed a number of Latin American countries back into the hands of just those forces of dictatorship, populism and corruption from which they were liberated for democracy only a few years ago. In the 1960s Latin America fell into the hands of the dictators because of the threat of communism from the East. In the 1990s the same may happen because of the burden debt from the West.

We simply cannot afford to leave this issue in the hands of the banks. If democracy is to survive in Latin America, and in other debtor nations, the governments of the West must take action to relieve the burden of debt.

Currency Instability

The debt burden has always rightly been identified as one of the most destabilising factors in the global ecomomy. But we have also underestimated the effect of the international currency market. The increasing velocity of the world economy go-round already has the potential to create instability which can unseat even powerful Western industrial nations.

Young people sit in Tokyo, New York and London, eyes glued to green screens, hands on keyboards and ears to their phones. These are the new gnomes of the international money markets. Altogether they now propel around the system a sum of money said to be thirty two times greater than is needed to finance the trade it is supposed to be there to support.

At the time of the last election we in the Alliance believed that the advent of a new government in Britain in which the financial market might not have immediate confidence would, almost overnight, devalue the nation's currency. It could make it impossible for a democratically elected party to fulfil its manifesto promises. That was the threat then. It is even greater now, with the pound unsupported by EMS membership and vulnerable to a rising trade deficit. Put simply, the money changers are now so powerful that they undermine the economic sovereignty and even democratic processes of the state.

No single economy can face this problem on its own. In that sense, there can be no Bretton Woods, because the world economy is now too powerful for any one economy to hold the ring as the US was able to do in the mid-1940s. It will need the world's most powerful economies to work in concert to do the job.

The only question is which comes first, the catastrophe or the solution?

The Group of 7, the world's most powerful economies should urgently step up their co-ordination of economic policy with particular emphasis on working out, as soon as possible, an effective system for currency co-operation – a system capable of stabilising the world's financial markets.

Trans National Corporation

It is not just the money changers who have the power to de- stabilise governments. Many trans-national corporations (TNCo) (multinationals, if you wish) now have 'GDPs' and budgets bigger than some developed nations. (General Motors has a 'GDP' of $14 billion, compared with Luxembourg which has a GDP little more than a third of this and Ecuador with a GDP of $10.3 billion. Indeed, there are no less than 67 countries in the world which have GDPs smaller than that of General Motors.)

The power of the TNCs is vast, growing and will have to be controlled. There are many of them who behave honourably and benignly, but there are many more who are just as exploitative and 'imperialistic' as the old European colonialists. No decent policy for the development of the Third World, for the protection of the world's natural resources and environment or for the stability of the world's economy can be complete if it does not tackle the issue of a code of practice for trans national corporations.

The Fragile Earth

Finally, perhaps the greatest threat of all is the threat to our global environment: how to combat the erosion and potential destruction of our fragile living space. And 'our' does not just mean us in Britain, or us in Europe, or us in the West. It means all of us, in whichever corner of the globe we happen to live. The problems which face us are large, international and potentially devastating.

If we cannot stop the destruction of the ozone layer, life itself on earth will become impossible. If we cannot halt the process of global warming, the lives of our grandchildren will be miserable and potentially very dangerous. If we cannot stop the pollution of our seas, lakes and rivers, then the world will be immeasurably more ugly and much more poisonous. If we cannot halt the proliferation of nuclear weapons or face up to the potential international hazards created by nuclear power, we could literally end up by destroying life itself.

There is no way that we can combat any of these threats if we remain stuck with Victorian notions of sovereignty and hold to the model of the nation state in the structure of world affairs. That is why it was very encouraging to hear President Gorbachov recently argue for a strengthening of the UN.

The United Nations has seen a bitter couple of decades. I worked there as a British diplomat in the mid-1970s and it was a pretty depressing experience. In the era of superpower politics, the UN has been relegated to the passive role of the bystander. All that must now change as we create a new and more hopeful climate in world affairs. It must change if we are to find the means to ensure that nations work together to confront the problems which threaten us all.

Internationalism should be the corner stone of Britain's foreign policy. We must provide a firm commitment to work with our partners in Western Europe for closer international co-operation and more effective international institutions. That is the only way to maintain an open and prosperous global economy, and a prosperous Britain within it. It is the only way to achieve a more peaceful and secure Europe. It is the only way to tackle the desperate problems of global pollution and environmental threat.

Conclusion

'Come to the edge', he said. They said 'We are afraid'. 'Come to the edge', he said. They came. He pushed them. And they flew.

Guillaume Apollinaire

It is more normal to put your beliefs at the beginning of a book, than at the end. But this book has been deliberately written as an 'agenda'. It is not intended as a statement of philosophical belief. Nevertheless, at the heart of it lies the conviction that sustains me in politics. It is not a new belief but it is constantly reinforced by every experience and observation I have on the exercise of power.

It is that a society cannot be free and is very unlikely to be successful for long unless the men and women in it have real power to determine their own destiny. The one thing that unfailingly gives me satisfaction in politics is to watch those who have been taught they are the subject of other's power, rise to meet the challenge of power in their own hands – and then be unbelieving at what they are able to do. To believe in this and make it happen, is, for me, the great passion of politics.

And yet – politics provides another experience, too. It is, if you like, the hard bump of reality. It is contained in the old truth that one man's freedom is all too often used to fashion another man's chains (and they usually ARE men, too).

And so I am forced to return to the humbling conclusion that mine is not a new thought, merely another formulation of the old riddle at the centre of democracy – where, in a free and just society, is the meeting point between liberty and restraint? There are no perfect answers to this – nor even are there answers which necessarily extend from one time to another or one place to a different one. This is just as well. For otherwise we should all have to believe in 'isms', and the world has had quite enough of those already.

In the end, therefore, the best we can do is propose a solution to the riddle for our time and place. That has been the aim of the book. I believe that there is a new and better society struggling to be born in Britain, in Europe and in this small planet we all share.

The purpose of this agenda for a Citizens' Britain is to set out some ways in which democratic politics might help that birth.